What People Are Saying About
BE UNACCEPTABLE

"Be Unacceptable is a brave and deeply personal journey into the psyche. Alex Harvey's honesty is raw, unguarded, and offered with a genuine intention to help readers recognise their own inner landscapes. Insightful, grounding, and deeply inspiring, Be Unacceptable is an invitation to look within and move beyond the layers of conditioning that no longer serve us."
— Dr. Alla Demutska, clinical psychologist & clinical director of counselling and psychotherapy

"Be Unacceptable gives language to everything we've been told to silence. It's bold, clear, and wildly liberating. This is the kind of book that changes how you see yourself — and what you believe you're allowed to become."
— Arja Hendrikx, international tantra teacher & speaker

"This isn't another feel-good typical empowerment book that leaves you on a short-term high. It's a FULL body activation. A fierce, embodied guide that blends deep, feminine truth with practical, tangible codes to step into your next level and highest self. To every woman who's ever felt "too much" or "not enough" and she's ready to embrace her truest self unapologetically.... You need

BE UNACCEPTABLE

this book immediately."
— Madeline Kossin, business mentor & 7-figure CEO

"Alex takes complex manifestation principles and makes them sassy, grounded, and easy to digest. Highly recommend."
— Clare Elizabeth Dea, speaker, performer & author

"A literary shake to the shoulders that will have you laughing, blushing, and waking the f up! Call me unacceptable or don't call me at all — the good girl is officially dead."
— Ellie Ann Deighton, author, poet & creative mentor

Be Unacceptable

Dare to live the life you're meant for.

Alex Harvey

Published by Temple of the Feminine Press
First edition December 2025

© Alex Harvey, 2025
All rights reserved.

No part of this publication may be reproduced, stored in a retrieval system, or transmitted in any form or by any means — electronic, mechanical, photocopying, recording, or otherwise — without prior written permission from the publisher.

The opinions expressed in this book are those of the author and do not represent the views of any institution or organisation.

This book is intended for informational and reflective purposes only and is not a substitute for professional psychological, medical, or legal advice.

A catalogue record for this book is available from the National Library of Australia.

ISBN: 978-1-7643740-0-2

Cover design: Alex Harvey
Illustrations: Alex Harvey
Author Photo: Ulrike Reinhold

*When I let go of who I think I am and who I think I need to be,
I become who I was born to be.*

— Alex Harvey

Dedication

This book is my offering to the feminine.

May we rise.

Contents

Preface: From Passion to the Pit of Doom	xii
Before We Begin	xv
PART ONE: Spells of Submission	1
Introduction	3
SPELL ONE: "There's Something Wrong with You"	13
SPELL TWO: Good Girl Conditioning	33
SPELL THREE: Permission	55
SPELL FOUR: Witch Wound	63
Seeing the Spells Speak	85
Part One Closing	91

PART TWO: The Divinely Wild Path of Being Unacceptable   93

   Introduction   95

   CODE ONE: The Holy Hot Service of Self-Worship   99

   CODE TWO: Feel Unworthy & Do It Anyway   111

   CODE THREE: Celebrate How Gloriously Wrong You Are   121

   CODE FOUR: You Are the Permission You've Been Waiting For   137

   CODE FIVE: Eat Your Fucking Fear For Breakfast   147

   CODE SIX: Tone It Up   157

The Be Unacceptable Codes   165

Your Next Dare: The Be Unacceptable 30-Day Challenge   167

Book Closing   171

Epilogue: The Unacceptable Path   173

Preface
From Passion to the Pit of Doom

HERE'S SOMETHING YOU MIGHT RELATE to.

I call it, *from passion to the pit of doom*.

I love to conceptualise things — it's definitely a kink.

It gets me so hot, bothered, and turned on that I can't sleep.

It goes something like this:

I'll have some positively electric vision or creative download — I'm SO excited about it. I feel lit up, full of passion and optimism, seeing endless possibilities *popping* in my mind's eye.

I then totally get off on writing down my *genius idea*, mapping out the vision, planning it, naming it — the full *visiongasm* shebang.

I'm in hot, *hot* heaven. Drunk on it.

There's no way this won't work — the world is going to go crazyyyyy for it, omggggg.

But when it comes time to *actually* do those things?

To write the actual content?
To record the videos?
To finalise, decide, and do?

My brain, body, and creativity lock up.

All of a sudden, it all feels wrong.

I don't know what to say. I don't know what to do.

Quite frankly, I feel sick. *This was a seriously bad idea.*

It all felt so clear and flowing during my concept phase — but now?

My mind has gone blank, and a ball of panic is forming in my stomach — I want to melt into the floor or cancel the whole thing.

In the scenario that I've already committed to this visiongasm project in some capacity, I actually want to vomit —

Why the fuck did I do that?? This is going to be so horrible, but I'll just have to get through it somehow — and then I will never do "this" to myself again.

The high hopes and fantasies of how groundbreaking this creation was going to be, and how right, true, and inevitable it felt in my body...

... suddenly all come crashing down, and I'm faced with the reality of how incomplete, incompetent, not ready, not good enough, and downright unworthy I feel.

How did that happen?

How did it happen, indeed — and what on earth can you do about it?

This question is what I've spent the last ten years of my life uncovering — as both a coach and humble seeker myself of my true path in life.

I wanted to understand — why isn't it all ease and magic to step onto and live my soul path? Wasn't it meant to be? Why does it stir up feelings of pain and wrongness worse than I've ever felt? Why do I hold back and pull back on the things I *know* are my purpose? What are the spells that bind us — and how do we break them?

The first five of those ten years?

I was powerless to this process.

When the crashing down moment detailed above came, I'd either get too stuck in my head to move forward, shrink the vision to something smaller and safer, or convince myself it wasn't a good idea anyway — off to die in the *genius idea graveyard*.

And I know I'm not the only one, because when women first come to me, I see the same *passion to the pit of doom* cycle playing out in their lives.

And when it does?

The *genius idea graveyard* has a fucking field day — all those incredible, awesome, divine, life-changing, could-have-been things go to *die*. Never to see the light of day.

If it were just about those ideas never being created, it might not be such a big deal, but it's much, *much* bigger than that.

Those ideas are the breadcrumbs of your true path — the path of fulfilling your soul's purpose and becoming the powerful, influential, self-realised woman you were born to be.

When those ideas go to die or get shelved for another five years?

So does the life you're meant for.

This book is my contribution to putting a stop to that.

You were born to shine, my dear, I know it, *and you know it too*.

It's the reason you picked up this book.

You were born to make a change in the world — to share your brilliance.

You were born to offer the world what only you can — the work that makes your heart come alive.

This isn't a book about feeling good — it's a book about remembering who the fuck you are and daring to live the life you're meant for.

Before We Begin

BEFORE WE DIVE IN, I want to clear a few things up so you know exactly how to read and benefit from this book.

A Note on Style

In a world of AI, and a world where not many people read novels anymore, it feels necessary to say this. You'll notice I use a lot of em dashes — these long lines that create rhythm and flow in the text.

They're not a sign that ChatGPT wrote this book. They're actually the *correct* form of dash in writing. (Fun fact: a hyphen, the short dash, is only meant to be used to hyphenate words. If you pick up almost any book, you'll see the long ones — the "em dashes".)

I love them because they mirror how I actually speak — with pauses, pivots, and bursts of thought. So when you see them everywhere, it's not AI — it's just me, writing the way I talk.

Premises

The ideas I present in this book are *premises* — working assumptions about how something works. The idea is that when you apply them, they yield the results you want. That's the only thing that matters.

Nothing I share can be proven as absolute fact — and I'm not asking you to *believe* any of it. These aren't beliefs. They're frameworks. Tools.

So as you read, you don't need to stress about whether you "agree" with all the ideas as I present them, or whether they line up perfectly with your current worldview. You don't have to be sold on any of it. You only have to apply the premises I offer wholeheartedly and see what happens. *Does it take you closer to the life you want to be living than your current way of living does?*

For me personally, these premises feel deeply true and resonant — but that's irrelevant. What matters is the empowerment, freedom, and results they unlock when you put them into practice.

Which brings me to the central premise of this book.

Central Premise

You have *Greatness* within you — and with it, a unique contribution you're here to make to the world. In other words: *your calling*.

When you follow your calling and live as an expression of your Greatness, you unlock the deepest fulfilment life has to offer *and* the most meaningful impact only you can create. Living this way brings a peace, joy, and success beyond what you could even imagine, because it flows from the truth of who you are.

Not only is this the path to the most rewarding life you can live — one in full alignment with your true nature — it's also the path to fulfilling your highest potential and offering your greatest gifts to the world.

This book is here to help you live that life — which I know matters to you more than anything.

Stories in This Book

All stories shared in this book are included with permission. Some names and identifying details have been changed to honour the privacy of the women whose stories are told.

I am deeply grateful to every woman who has allowed me to share a piece of her journey in these pages. In offering her story, she not only serves this book — she serves you and the collective rise of women remembering their power.

A Note on Language

As you read, you'll notice I use words like *heart, soul, true nature, true self, higher self, creative spirit, genius,* and *Greatness* somewhat interchangeably. To me, they're all facets of the same essence — the deepest truth of who you are and what you're here to bring.

I define your purpose as the expression of that essence in the world — both the life you uniquely desire to live in every facet, and the contribution you're uniquely designed to give.

Don't get caught up wondering if they mean different things. Think of them as different doorways into the same room. Each has its own flavour, and I use them for rhythm and resonance. Different words land with different people — so my intention is that by weaving them all through this book, it will awaken in you the truth I'm pointing at.

Definitions of Acceptable & Unacceptable in This Book

These two words — *acceptable* and *unacceptable* — are the foundation of this book. So let's be clear about what they mean here.

When I use the word *acceptable*, I don't just mean "socially polite" or "following the rules". I mean the deep conditioning we all receive about exactly how we *should* (or *shouldn't*) be in order to count as a valid human being and be enabled to have what we want.

To be *acceptable* is:

- To make yourself likeable.

- To shrink yourself so you don't take up too much space.

- To tone it down so you don't upset, offend, or create conflict.

- To contort yourself into whatever shape wins approval or permission.

- To silence your deepest loves and desires, believing you have to earn the right to them — or that they're simply not valid or okay, ever.

- To become anything other than exactly who you are, doing what lights you up.

When you're *acceptable*? You feel like your soul is dying.

When I use the word *unacceptable*, I mean the opposite.

To be *unacceptable* is:

- To step outside the internalised rules you've been living by.

- To unapologetically take up space.

- To let your full passion and energy flow.

- To shine, even when it makes others uncomfortable.

- To do what you'd love, exactly as you most love to do it, right now.

- To live raw. To live real. To live free of needing external validation to do or anything.

- To stand fully in who you are — no matter who or what you believe it threatens.

When you're *unacceptable*? You're *unstoppable*.

Sound like something you want to unlock?

Let's dive innnnn, bish.

PART ONE
Spells of Submission

The illusions that keep you small, safe, and acceptable.

Introduction

I'VE ATTEMPTED TO WRITE THIS book four times in the past two years.

It's actually more than that — because the first time, I went away for a week and restarted it at least four times *in that week*, only for every attempt to end up in the *genius-idea graveyard*.

And now, this attempt, is my *fifth restart* in one week. And if you're reading this, it was my fifth and *final*. Thank god. Talk about resistance.

Each time I've restarted, I get almost to the end of the first chapter before stopping.

Is it because I just really like writing introductions and opening chapters?

No.

I mean, I do love writing those things, but I would love to write a whole book, thanks.

The reason I keep stopping at the end of Chapter One is this:

The illusion that exactly what I want to write, and how I want to write it isn't okay, enough, or *right.*

I start the book all bright-eyed and bushy-tailed, and then I stop — not because I don't want to keep going, but because that's when everything suddenly starts to feel wrong.

Why, you might ask? If it's in alignment, shouldn't I have no resistance? Shouldn't it be blissfully easy?

Absolutely not. That's the first myth we'll be busting in this book.

The reason is this: once I get started, the unconscious tension between my vision and my beliefs begins to rise — hijacking my focus.

That tension automatically starts pulling my attention away from the end result I see for the book and placing it squarely on everything my conditioning says isn't okay about it.

So, this morning, when I wanted to scrap my latest draft again, I decided it was time to dig a little deeper and get to the bottom of this pattern that was now so obviously playing out.

Here's exactly what I wrote in my journal as I took myself through that process:

> *I keep getting stuck with this book because I'm afraid my mentor will read it and think it's both rubbish and flat out wrong, because I've presented*

> my own ideas and not just shared exactly what I've been taught, as I was taught.
>
> I need to explain everything to the nth degree and be able to indisputably prove it — and I need everyone in the world who I can imagine reading this book to agree with me — I need to present it in a way that my ideas are indisputable by anyone.
>
> On the other hand I assume that no one needs to hear any of this anyway or needs anything from me, because they're all sorted and perfect. I assume that what I'm writing about isn't actually a real struggle for anyone else, so I just sound like an idiot and no one cares.
>
> Not only that, but I need to explain how every single thing I mention works, where it comes from, and somehow through that, explain the mechanisms of the entire Universe.

Pretty tall order.

Now, here's what I want to highlight — I wasn't consciously thinking these things.

In my conscious mind, I was picturing the woman I was writing this for, but it was just starting to feel all wrong.

Unconsciously, *the voice of acceptable* was silently seeping into my consciousness, draining my creative energy and lulling me to sleep, like a deadly gas I couldn't see, pulling me straight toward…

You know where...

Dun dun dunnnn.

The pit of doom.

It was casting a spell — whispering that I had to fix myself and line up perfectly in all the ways I'd written in my journal (most of which aren't even possible!) before I was allowed to write this book.

It had so seamlessly seduced me into believing that the way I am, and what I want to write, is simply *not acceptable.*

Way back at the start of my personal development journey, I was taught that this kind of thing was just my own limiting beliefs — ones I could change by simply "choosing new ones" to believe.

But over the years, I learned that limiting beliefs aren't just thoughts you can swap out for shinier ones at will. They're rooted deep in the psyche — in the conditioning each of us learned about what it means to be acceptable in life and the world.

And your ego? It's absolutely committed to abiding by that conditioning — it's the compass it uses to navigate life.

That's what I call the *voice of acceptable.*

It's why you're here, reading this book.

You have it too.

INTRODUCTION

Despite your best efforts to get out there and slayyyy — to be that mf powerhouse woman who doesn't care what anyone think, carves her own path, and says "fuck the rules, yo" — there's another part of you desperate to please, fit in, and stay *very* acceptable to the world.

That's why you can't fully step into your next level, hold it, or embody it the way you crave — not once you step outside the safety of your bedroom and into the real world, anyway.

Because deep down, you already know: the biggest thing standing between you and the next level you want so badly... *is you.*

And yet, here you still are.

It's maddening, isn't it?

Fortunately, this book is here to help you with that — once and for all.

Here's what I want you to know: it's not because of any personal failing.

It's not because you're not motivated enough, too lazy, not good enough, not worthy, or not one of the *chosen ones*...

It's because you have a voice in your head telling you that you absolutely must be acceptable before you can do the thing — and right now, *you're not.*

And that voice?

It's not just a far-off voice in your head — it has a full-access pass to your operating system: the code that runs your thoughts, feelings, and choices. Which means it has the power to completely overwhelm and *dominate you*.

And it doesn't come from nowhere — it's born of the spells you've been under since the day you got here.

Those are what we're going to break together.

So rest assured, you're not *super fucked up* because you experience this; you've just never been taught how to turn the tables and *dominate this voice instead*.

That's about to change.

Women are absolutely stuffed to the eyeballs with every standard and measure they've been told they need to meet in order to be acceptable to the world — many of which completely contradict each other.

Talk about a minefield.

Every day, I work closely with women to bring their deepest dreams to life — in my courses, at my retreats, with my 1:1 clients, and even in the emails in my inbox.

And from all of them, I hear the same thing:

The endless ways they feel like they don't measure up yet — like they're not getting everything right, and that's the problem.

INTRODUCTION

Beneath it all runs the same deep, delusional belief: that they're simply not enough to have their dreams.

Pretty enough.
Skinny enough.
Fit enough.
Smart enough.
Capable enough.
Charismatic enough.
Cool enough.
Extroverted enough.
Successful enough.
Show-stoppingly amazing enough.
Together enough.
In control enough.
Fashionable enough.
Rich enough.
Neat enough.
Disciplined enough.
Motivated enough.
Qualified enough.
Popular enough.
Confident enough.
Attractive enough.
Secure enough.
Self-believing enough.
Good enough.

There's this nagging sense that they're not getting life right yet — that they're failing in some capacity, and that's the problem.

If they could just get it all right, do more, and be completely perfect, then everything would finally come together.

Sound familiar?

And these aren't women on the sidelines of life. They're smart, talented, creative, capable, stunning, funny, and exceptional — *just like you.*

They have everything going for them — *you have everything going for you* — which is why it makes zero fucking sense when they shrink back instead of showing up in their full brilliance.

Yet over and over, they find themselves pulling back and shrinking instead of shining.

And as a result?

The books never get written.
The courses never get made.
The innovative designs never come to life.
The art collects dust in the basement.
The people's lives don't get transformed.
The genius new modalities never get created.
The apps never get launched.
The magical tinctures never get shared.

All of it — dumped straight into the *genius idea graveyard*.

A graveyard overflowing with world-changing visions, creative downloads, and life-altering brilliance that never saw the light of day — all because women kept waiting to feel enough before claiming what was already theirs to take.

Brutal, right?

If you don't learn how to break into your own operating system and take the fucking wheel back from the voice of acceptable, it's the life you'll end up living, along with many before you.

INTRODUCTION

One of the most toxic quotes that goes around the internet is this:

What's meant for you will never pass you by.

This is absolute bullshit.

Everything that's meant for you will pass you by if you're too afraid to rock the boat, risk everything, face down the screaming voice of acceptable, and claim it.

Anyone who's absolutely grabbed life by the balls knows that it's 100% a choice — and it's a choice most people are simply too afraid to make.

Why?

Because being *tamed* feels so much safer than being free.

And because *the voice of acceptable* doesn't show up yelling, "I'm your conditioning!"

It whispers, *"I'm just being realistic. This is what's safe. It's common sense."*

But not you.

You're here to break the spell and claim your life back.

And I'm here to help you do it.

So let's fucking get in there, get dirty, and come out with your gold.

In Part One, we're breaking down *the spells that bind you — the illusions that keep you small, safe, and acceptable.*

These spells are why people-pleasing, perfectionism, toning it down, or feeling unworthy keep sneaking back in — even after ten ayahuasca ceremonies.

You didn't fail — you just never saw the full scope of what was really going on. Once you do? You'll have the power to step up, step out, and live the life you're meant for.

Ready?

SPELL ONE
"There's Something Wrong with You"

The illusion that you need fixing
— and why you'll never feel like enough.

AT THE HEART OF THE *"There's Something Wrong with You" Spell* ... is the *gaping hole of not-enoughness.*

We're starting with the deepest one.

The good news is, we all have it.

The other good news is, it doesn't actually mean anything about you — it's not real, it's just an *illusion* your mind projects, a sensation that feels convincing but isn't true.

This is the first way we start shaping ourselves to be *acceptable* — by believing we need to make up for something we lack.

So, *why the hell does it feel so real and convincing?*

Because you, my love, are not only an infinitely powerful soul with a burning mission — you also have an ego.

If you're not super familiar with the term *ego*, let me define what it refers to in spiritual and philosophical contexts.

When I say *ego*, I don't mean arrogance — I mean the survival-oriented part of you that constantly scans for danger and fixates on potential threats.

On a primal level, as much as survival depends on food and shelter, it also depends on *belonging*. Your brain still thinks a lion might eat you if you get thrown out of the tribe — that's how deep the need to belong runs.

Here's where it starts: between the ages of zero and five, the role of your ego was to build an identity — to figure out who you are, how the world works, and what you need to do to survive within it.

At its core, it was trying to answer — *who am I, and who do I have to be to get love, validation, and belonging here?*

The conclusions it drew from those early experiences became your operating system — the rules it believes you must follow to exist safely in the world.

And there's one key thing your ego has always been scanning for — one thing it believes your survival depends on: *validation.*

In your identity-building phase, your ego sought two forms of proof that you, and your pure creative nature, are valid:

   1. That you belong in the world.

> 2. That it's safe to bring your heart — your true nature and gifts — into the world.

It sought the first from your mother and the second from your father.

Your psyche looked to your mother to answer the question: *Do I belong here?*

And it looked to your father to answer the question: *Is it safe to be me in the world, will my heart be received?*

No matter how loving or terrible your parents were, no one receives 100% validation.

It's impossible.

You inevitably experienced moments where your ego perceived that your true self wasn't welcomed, accepted, allowed, or safe — whether this was completely imagined or very real.

And what did your ego do when that happened?

It interpreted it as a threat to your very existence — proof that something is wrong with you, and that to survive, you must compensate for it.

And that's where it began — your sense of separation.

The fall from grace — the moment you stopped knowing you were pure divinity.

No longer feeling at one with life itself.

The wound against your true nature — the wound every human carries.

In other words — *I'm not acceptable as I am.*

This is the origin of the human illusion — the part of you that would spend a lifetime trying to fix what was never broken.

With *ego* defined, let's start unpacking this spell.

The "There's Something Wrong with You" Spell.
The illusion that you need fixing — and why you'll never feel like enough.

This is the spell your ego has been casting since childhood — the one that makes you chase wholeness like it's something you lost.

Since your ego equates not being validated with death, it believes your life is about becoming who it thinks you need to be to finally win the love or recognition you never got — to be the one who belongs, who's important, special, worthy, capable… or whichever flavour of *not enough* your ego is programmed to run.

This is why the *gaping hole of not-enoughness* feels so real: to your ego, if you don't fix it, you will die. You won't make it. You won't be okay.

So it goes on, forever projecting your childhood experience onto life — whispering, *see? This is just like before. You're not enough. You're not safe. There's something wrong with you.*

What I want you to see is this:

It's the very nature of your ego to feel that *gaping hole of not-enoughness*.

It's not *you*. It's nothing personal. It's just the nature of a part of your psyche. And as such, it will never stop — and it doesn't need to.

For instance, maybe your father never truly saw your talent or abilities — and your ego concluded that the world doesn't see them either. So now, no matter what recognition you get, the same old feeling returns: *No one really sees me. No matter what I do, it's never enough.*

Or maybe your mother didn't come when you cried at night — and your ego decided you don't belong, that you're alone, and that if you don't figure it all out yourself, you'll die. So now, no matter how many friends you have or how much support surrounds you, the same old feeling returns: *No one wants me. I don't belong. I'm not going to be okay.*

These stories and sensations have nothing to do with what's happening now — they're just your ego projecting the meanings it formed in childhood onto your present-day circumstances trying to make sense of what's happening and what you need to do to survive.

And these meanings? They *feel* like a threat to your very existence.

Your ego never got the memo that your childhood conditions are over — it still assumes what happened then is what life will always be.

Ouch.

This is the root of your most fundamental limiting beliefs — formed in those early experiences of unmet validation.

So, inside you, there are *two* powerful forces:

1. Your ego — the wounded image, obsessed with fixing what it thinks is broken.

2. Your pure creative spirit — your true essence, burning to create, shine, and share your gifts.

One is survival. The other is truth.

Let me show you this in action.

A big challenge I've faced throughout my life — one that's been ever-present and dominating in my business journey — is feeling deeply unworthy and full of shame, for no real apparent reason.

It's often completely delusional — but it has crippled me in the past, nonetheless.

I remember the first time it hit me like a sledgehammer.

It was just over ten years ago, and I was about six months into my first coaching business.

Coaching was something that had found me in a way, and I had discovered I was really good at it. I felt incredibly passionate and purposeful doing it — and, thanks to the internet, had delusionally high hopes about how easy and fast it would be to build a business.

Six months in, I had spent all of my *runway savings* from my engineering job and I wasn't earning even close to a consistent income yet through my business.

In reality?

This is really normal and there was nothing wrong.

All I needed to do was keep going, keep figuring out what I was doing, keep figuring out my message, just try stuff, and supplement my income with a job while I did that.

Super simple. No sweat.

Except that *I was sweating!*

To my ego, I should be immediately *successful* and earning a lot of money to validate that I was worthy of my pursuit. I believed that if I wasn't earning a lot of money, it proved I wasn't enough or wanted by the world.

So when my money ran out and I wasn't raking it in, my brain decided it meant *there was something wrong with me.*

Oh my God, I'm not ok. This isn't working. What's wrong with me?

These thoughts had absolutely *zero* grounding in reality and everything to do with my ego freaking out because it believed I lacked the validation I needed to survive.

What happened next?

Stricken with a terror that was completely made up in my brain, I slid mercilessly into the *pit of doom*.

Instead of functionally looking at the situation, getting a job, and continuing to follow my path with passion and determination to serve women through coaching...

I melted into a spiral of shame. I convinced myself I was such a freak of nature that I wouldn't even be able to get a job anymore — and completely retreated from sharing my coaching.

The result?

Within a couple of months, I was on the brink of a total breakdown — and I quit my business.

I quit.

Sound familiar?

That moment when you get so lost in your head — under the crushing weight of *I'm not enough* or *there's something wrong with me* — that you just can't go on, so you give up on your dream?

I was going down that hole. Not because of anything real, but because my childhood wound of unmet validation was being projected onto my current reality — and my ego was convinced it meant I wasn't okay. That I wasn't going to make it.

Straight into the *genius idea graveyard* my business went — another bold, bright vision laid to rest before it ever had a chance.

And once again, the *"There's Something Wrong with You" Spell* was in full force.

There was no problem — the entire thing was in my head.

After weeks of waking up in tears every morning, I was desperate to feel smart, impressive, and recognised again.

I was craving that "V".

So I thought, *why don't I study law next — go on exchange to Oxford?*

That would make me feel good about myself.

I was prostituting my life path to feel successful, and I knew it — but I didn't care.

I just wanted that *gaping hole of not-enoughness* to go away and this, I thought, was my golden ticket to being *acceptable* again.

While I waited for the next law entrance exams, coaching wasn't done with me.

Feeling traumatised by the crash and burn of my experience attempting to start a coaching business, when it came knocking on my door again, I timidly answered the call.

This time? I had people asking me to help them with money — the inner work and outer work.

I swore to myself this time, *I will support this business until it supports me.*

This slow, gentle approach was going okay — until I decided to go all in again.

I had created a course and had about 20 people go through it and love it. So I thought to myself, *how about I do a "proper" marketing campaign to launch this course?*

So, I bought a course about how to do that and created a carefully planned strategy. Not only that, I invested a large chunk of my savings to have someone set up a funnel and run Facebook ads for me.

I then worked my tooshie off crafting the *perfect* webinar, writing the *perfect* email sequence, and presenting as the *perfect* person people would want to learn from.

This cannot NOT work, I thought with pleasure and excitement.

How very humbled I was.

After the first webinar I ran, one person signed up — and the next morning, they asked for a refund.

In that moment, it felt like the world — and all my fantasies of success — came crashing down on me.

And rising up to meet me was the hot, hot shame of my *perceived* utter wrongness.

And guess what? The same loop as before came rushing back — the same words, the same fear — déjà vu in my own mind.

The *"There's Something Wrong with You" Spell* was back. In full force.

Oh my god, I'm not okay. This is not working. What's wrong with me?

The reality?

You guessed it — there was nothing wrong.

It was all an illusion in my head. The course wasn't even starting for another three weeks. And the number of sign-ups wasn't a reflection of my value or what I had to share anyway.

But to me?

The fact no one had signed up yet was proof that there was not only something deeply wrong with me, but also, *that I would never make it in life because of it.*

I can't tell you how badly I wanted my existence to end then and there.

Stricken with this intense shame, I, yet again, retreated from even promoting the upcoming course — threatening it, and everything that would come after it, with the *genius idea graveyard*.

Fortunately, I got some coaching, woke the hell up, and got my shit together.

I threw out my "perfectly crafted" strategy, got real about how I could connect with the people in my audience who would benefit from the course, and invited them onto calls to discuss it.

One week later?

I kicked off the course with ten amazing humans, helping them all change their relationship to money and set up systems that would change their lives. I made $11,000, which was a total first for me and a huge business achievement.

All because I woke up from the delusional spiral my ego would have had me go down, and stayed true to my vision.

Now, I wish I could tell you that this was the last time it happened, that I realised my power, never to be tricked again — but not only would that be a big fat lie, but it also wouldn't help you.

If I said that? All it would do is make you feel even more fucked up the next time the terrifying feeling of *I'm not-okay* seeps in, yet again, when you thought you "had healed it already".

And I'm here to break the spell — not reinforce it.

You will feel it again. Over and over.

The total delusion that what you're thinking, feeling, or experiencing means anything about you.

Here's what you need to know: it doesn't mean anything about you. *There is nothing wrong with you.* You're not behind. You're not wrong. You're not a failure. You're not unlovable. You're not unimportant. You're not useless. You're not incapable.

Whatever it's telling you — isn't real. It's a childhood projection of what you believe this experience must mean.

Just like there was absolutely nothing wrong with me in either of the scenarios I just shared with you.

There was nothing wrong with me, I just made it mean that, then spiralled, and then reinforced the belief through my withdrawal.

During all of this, I was doing a lot of "healing work" on myself. There were so many times I thought I'd cracked it. I'd have a breakthrough, feel light and free, convinced I was finally done with the pain and dysfunction.

And then — the same pit of doom would open beneath me, again.

But here's the thing: when it did, it felt even worse. Because I thought I'd already healed it, the only conclusion my mind could draw was: *I must be even more broken than I thought. I must be really fucked up.*

God damn.

That's what the fix-yourself world of personal development does to people — it's toxic.

You might feel better for a moment — riding the emotional high of catharsis — but when the feeling you thought you'd "healed" inevitably returns, you end up feeling even more fucked up than before. Because now, you're also convinced you're failing at healing.

You start to think maybe you'll never make it to that promised land where everything's finally sorted — where life just magically works out — and that you're doomed to stay stuck in this hell forever.

Which, obviously, your ego concludes... is all you deserve anyway.

"Healing" has A LOT to answer for.

The ironic twist of the *"There's Something Wrong with You" Spell* is this: the more you try to heal it away, the more *unacceptable* you feel when it comes back.

When really, the truth is: all you have to do is wake up and stop believing it.

This spell doesn't show up the same way for everyone — it wears different masks, depending on how your validation was unmet in childhood and what your ego decided that meant.

In my training, I learned a model describing twelve fundamental beliefs the ego can form from this sense of incompleteness. I find this brilliant and use it in my work.

But for the sake of this book, rather than take you through all twelve, I've found that five of them show up most consistently and deeply in women — shaped by the conditioning we've inherited about what's acceptable, how we're meant to behave, and the limits of our power.

These five core delusions are the root of patterns of self-doubt, shame, and making yourself small.

I call them *The Five Core Ego Delusions.*

You'll recognise every one of them.

The Five Core Ego Delusions

1. The *I'm Unworthy* Delusion

Feels like: You're bad at your core and must keep proving you're good enough to deserve love.

Shows up as: Overgiving, undercharging, feeling bad whenever someone does something for you or gives you something, people-pleasing to make up for how "bad" you secretly feel, feeling guilt or shame, seeking endless "healing".

Core lie: *There's something wrong with me and it makes me unlovable/ unworthy/ undeserving.*

2. The *I'm Not Enough* Delusion

Feels like: You're always one achievement, qualification, or milestone away from finally being whole, and then everything will come together.

Shows up as: Endless studying, hustling, fixated on getting somewhere in the future, chasing external success while never feeling satisfied, when you reach your goals — moving the goal post because it still doesn't feel like enough yet.

Core lie: *Once I achieve enough, I'll be valid.*

3. The *I'm Insignificant/ Invisible* Delusion

Feels like: No one truly sees your essence, your value, or the gifts you have to share.

Shows up as: Feeling like no matter how good you are — no one will see it, fixated on whether you're getting attention or not (e.g. not getting attention or engagement on social media sends you into a spiral), withdrawing when you don't get attention because *what's the point?*

Core lie: *I'm not seen, so nothing I do will have any impact.*

— ❖ —

4. The *I'm Not Allowed (to Be Powerful/ an Authority)* Delusion

Feels like: You'll be punished, rejected, or humiliated if you stand in authority or become powerful/ successful.

Shows up as: Finding yourself shrinking back after success, killing momentum somehow after you generate it, needing permission or validation before making decisions, fearing you'll overstep, feeling unexplained shame or fear for positioning yourself as an authority.

Core lie: *If I'm powerful, I'll be rejected — it's not my place, I'm not allowed.*

5. The *I Need to Be Perfect* Delusion

Feels like: You can't start or step into your brilliance until you've got every detail flawless.

Shows up as: Procrastination, harsh self-criticism, highly judgmental of others, holding relentlessly high standards for yourself and others, endless tweaking before sharing, never ready to start because it's not perfect yet.

Core lie: *I need to be perfect before I can create what I want.*

Any of these feelings and experiences sound familiar?

Whether you saw yourself in one of these delusions or all five, it doesn't make you any more or less fucked up.

These are simply the masks your ego wears, all flowing from the same *gaping hole of not-enoughness*, a feature of our humanity.

The sabotaging stories they seduce you with *aren't real*. Convincing, yes, but ultimately powerless once you see them for what they are.

This is how the *"There's Something Wrong with You" Spell* operates — not through any truth, but through convincing illusions that make you feel *unacceptable*.

The work isn't to fix them. It's to wake up and stop believing the stories.

Breaking the Spell — Reflection

- Take a moment to feel this one in your body.
- Which of these delusions grab you most strongly?
- What do they tell you is true about you?
- What do you *do* when they're screaming at you?

The next time you hear one of these voices, catch it. Name it. And remind yourself: *This is not truth, this is my ego — the echo of my childhood's unmet validation projected onto the present.*

Because when you stop believing the delusion, you stop feeding the spell, and you remember you were never unacceptable in the first place.

Now that we've seen through the *"There's Something Wrong with You" Spell*, we're going to peel back the next layer of illusion:

The cultural spell that taught you to be pleasing and nice.

To smile when you want to cry.

To say yes when you want to say no.

And above all else, to serve everyone else before yourself — to make yourself *acceptable* at any cost.

Let's talk about what you have to give up to break it.

SPELL TWO
Good Girl Conditioning

The illusion that you must be good
— and why it feels unsafe to be you.

WHILE EVERYONE DEVELOPS THEIR OWN *illusions of not-enoughness*, women face an additional, insidious layer of how they need to line up in life — this is the cultural conditioning of what it means to be a *good girl*.

It's a spell that's been cast for generations, teaching women to trade their truth for approval.

As we've established, your ego's entire job is to secure validation, because validation equals survival.

How do I need to appear to be accepted by the world?
What do I need to do, or not do?
What's okay, or not okay?

FYI — your soul isn't the one asking these questions. It already knows you're whole.

But to your ego, *there's a rule book.*

During your childhood, it was busy writing it — recording how the world works, your place in it, what's safe, and how you must be in order to belong.

At the centre of that book is one question: What is *good,* and what is *bad*?

Or, in other words, what is *acceptable* and what is *unacceptable* to maintain approval.

That's the foundation of the *acceptable identity* every woman learns to build — and the cage she must later break.

The rulebook most women come up with? It's endless.

How to look, how to speak, how much to give, how much to want, when to smile, when to shrink...

It's full of contradictions, ensuring that no matter what you do, you're breaking a rule somewhere.

Now, the truth is, our culture has operated under oppressive structures for women for thousands of years.

But we don't need to carry that as a heavy weight, or spend our lives raging against the patriarchy — in fact, doing so only keeps us entangled in the very energy we want to be free from.

The point of seeing this isn't to drown in it — it's to *liberate yourself* from it. To recognise the forces that shaped your psyche so you can reclaim your sovereignty.

Every human has the responsibility to free themselves from the internalised sense of limitation they've inherited — the control they continue to uphold in their own mind long after any real oppressor is gone.

The original system may have vanished generations ago — but the spell remains in your mind as long as you abide by it.

That's why we're here. Not to deny what's true, but to see it clearly — so you can take your power back.

And that brings us to...

The Good Girl Conditioning Spell.
The illusion that you must be good — and why it feels unsafe to be you.

Every woman alive today has been subject to it. It's built on centuries of messaging about what your role is and how you need to behave as a woman, in order to be allowed to exist in society.

This conditioning runs deep — it's the spell that makes women play small even when their soul is bursting to break free, take up space and create magic.

It's why so many women don't step up to lead their movements, shift industries, write their books, or claim their expertise — while men do, often without a second thought.

It's what keeps women waiting to be chosen, waiting to be perfect, and waiting to tick every box before daring to say, "*I can do that."* Meanwhile men with half the qualifications put up their hand — and get handed the mic.

It's the spell that teaches women to seek permission instead of power, and to master the art of being chosen rather than choosing themselves.

And nowhere does this spell bite harder than when a woman dares to own her power in the very realms she's been taught are *taboo*.

Early in my money coaching business, as I was developing my work, I ran into a conflict.

My first coaching business — the one I'd quit — had been about empowering women to reconnect with their pleasure and sexuality.

The wisdom and insight I passionately wanted to share came straight out of my own journey — finally discovering truths about the female body, about pleasure, and about sexual energy that blew my mind.

I'd discovered truths that were somehow hidden secrets off in the fringes of sexuality work, not even part of mainstream sexuality education.

It baffled me, bordering on outrage. *How on earth was this not common knowledge?*

What I discovered went far beyond sex — it was about personal power.

When women claimed their pleasure and tapped into their sexual energy, it wasn't just about better intimacy — it created an energetic shift that changed everything about how they moved through the world.

They *felt* their power, confidence, creativity, a remembrance of their infinite worth — and embodied it.

As I built my money coaching business, it felt like a disservice that I didn't obviously include this discovery I had made — I even had women in my audience who knew this was my coaching background and were *asking me* to include it in my work.

I wanted to. But the very thing I knew was most powerful for women was also the very thing my conditioning told me was *unacceptable*.

A voice in my head was saying, *if you mention pleasure or sexual energy, it will destroy your credibility.*

I remember telling a few friends:

"Because I'm talking about money, I feel like I have to show myself to be professional, polished, and above all — non-sexual. If I mention anything about sexuality, it will discredit my intelligence."

It felt like if I dared bring any mention of sexuality into my work, I'd be banished from respectable society — exiled to the fringes with the other freaks that didn't make the cut of being acceptable.

Was my fear of being discredited logical in a true sense?

No. Being sexual, or teaching deeper truths about our sexual nature, has nothing to do with intelligence — it's not like it makes your IQ go down...

But to my conditioning, and probably yours too? Sex, sexual pleasure, or being a sexual woman, is *bad* to talk about, reveal, or express openly.

It was an illusion, but in my ego's rule book — to be frank — that stuff was for *dumb girls who didn't have brains, morals, or self-respect.*

Ouch.

That hits *hard*. And no, I'm not sorry for the pun.

This is classic *Good Girl Conditioning*.

Here's another thing about *Good Girl Conditioning*: When it's a concept you're hooked into, it feels very real and very true, like, *these are the rules of society you must abide by, otherwise you won't be allowed in anywhere, or be allowed to have anything.* Sound reminiscent of being four years old?

Again, the truth is, *it's another illusion*.

When you stop believing these really are the rules of life, two things happen:

First, you realise most people aren't watching you as closely as you think — it was never as universal as your conditioning claimed.

Second — even more important — when you fully own yourself, you stop being *questionable* to people.

Ever notice those people who are kinda outrageous — absolutely unacceptable — and own the hell out of it? Ever notice how even the people you'd assume would judge them either don't care, or actually respect them for it?

Yeah, that's right.

When you don't subscribe to those rules anymore, you embody a certainty that makes you *undeniable*.

People don't blink or question you anymore, because you no longer question yourself. The only reason it ever felt like society was scrutinising you is because *you were still scrutinising you*.

That's the real spell.

It tricks you into doubting your own power, and in that doubt, you invite the world to mirror it back. But when you stop playing along, the illusion collapses — and suddenly, *you're free.*

Sure, some people might still judge you or reject you, but you just don't give a shit anymore, and you see it doesn't actually obstruct you from anything that truly matters to you.

There came a point I couldn't betray myself or the service I knew I was meant to give any longer.

So, slightly shaking, I started to introduce the sexual energy and pleasure practices into my work.

I also started to own myself as a sensual, sexual being in my business.

For me, that didn't mean lingerie photos though — it meant dressing how I wanted, dancing how I wanted, and allowing myself to be my full sensual self, even joking about how many glass dildos I should pack when I travelled.

Sure, it turned some people away. But for my soul tribe — the women meant for me — it made me magnetic. *The biggest turn-on.*

It became *the reason* women wanted to work with me.

It has now even led me to create my own line of artisan, goddess-worthy glass dildos — which women are lining up to buy.

Breaking free of *Good Girl Conditioning* allowed me to step into my purpose, my medicine, my genius — that is, *exactly what I'm here to do, and how I'm here to do it.*

The moment I stopped trying to be respectable, I found my calling, my passion, an endless wellspring of inspiration, and what I was really here to share.

If I didn't? I wouldn't be living the life I'm living right now.

My business would've died. I'd have been too busy conforming and trying to be acceptable — anxious, stuck, spiraling, and offering nothing truly unique or compelling.

I would have stayed in the land of the beige, destined to disappear into the beige background.

I know because I've been there!

I would eventually have had to admit defeat, take the safe job and settle for the sensible path — all because I couldn't let my authentic self take the wheel. All because I didn't believe it was a viable way to be.

90% of what I've achieved?

Would be in my motherfucking *genius idea graveyard*.

Quietly decaying.

What was meant for me in life?

Would be passing me by.

And it would have sucked. But fortunately, I found another route. And so can you.

You have a genius.

You are not vanilla, beige, forgettable or replaceable.

If you feel vanilla right now, it's not because you are, it's because your ego's rule book has decided your true nature is too much, too wild, or too wrong to show. So you did a good job at squashing it down and hiding it *even from your own view*.

You have an undeniable genius and that genius is a wellspring of ideas, creativity, and magnetic energy — it's something only *you* can express in your exact flavour and essence.

But you've been conditioned to believe that there's something wrong with it, so you hide, squash, and exile that very genius in order to be *acceptable*.

The very thing you're seeking, it's right there inside you, and you're just squashing it.

That — right there — is what's stopping you. That's why you keep experiencing lack and lacklustre results.

It's not because *you're not perfect enough yet*, it's because you're trying to line up perfectly with all the rules and not being yourself. You're so buried in it, you can't even see it. You don't even know anymore what your unique essence and gifts are, which you're denying.

This is normal, babe — *and it's why you're here reading this book.*

This is the journey of discovering your true self:

As you peel back the layers of the egoic identity that you've built, your true nature doesn't need to be invented — it simply reveals itself. It unfolds. And you experience just how sweet and sublime the real you truly is.

Did I know back when I felt the nudge to bring sexuality into my money business that it would eventually lead to creating glass pleasure toys, or a modality that uses sexual energy to awaken genius? *Absolutely not.*

Now that I'm doing it?

It feels so obvious — like there could be no other way.

That's what it will feel like for you too, as you meet yourself beyond the concepts of who you are and how you need to be in the world.

How truly unacceptable can I allow myself to be?

The more I do, the more my work thrives, the more things come together in magical and unexpected ways, the more magnetic I become, and the more peace and ease I feel knowing I'm living exactly the life I'm meant to be living.

The *Good Girl Conditioning Spell* is fucking big. And it's piled with endless rules.

To help you unpack it, I've broken it down into ten core "programs" that keep it in place.

Think of these as the sub-spells inside the bigger *Good Girl Conditioning Spell* — the ten rules that have been running your life without you even realising.

In doing so, you're going to see much more clearly why you're compelled to do certain behaviours you don't want to be doing, and why you feel blocked from stepping into the thing you want to step into.

When I started seeing how this conditioning had run my life, it was uncomfortable, and I felt grief seeing how I had betrayed myself and exiled my essence. But it was the only way through to claiming back every part of myself I'd given up and living the fully expressed life I get to live today.

You might feel this grief too as you read through these programs and feel the weight of what you've sacrificed. If you do, I want to encourage you to let yourself feel it, and at the same time, let yourself rejoice in the sweet relief of knowing you get to claim it all back, and what a wild and wonderful gift that is.

The moment you see these programs, you're no longer blindly living them.

Ready?

The 10 Good Girl Conditioning Programs

1. The *Don't Be Sexy or Sexual* Program

The spell in one line
This program convinces you that being sexy, sensual, or attractive is unsafe, shallow, or immoral.

Validated for
Being modest, pretending you don't care how you look, downplaying your attractiveness, and judging interest in

appearance as vain or shallow — while emphasising intelligence, humility, or hard work instead.

Judged for
Dressing sexy, walking into a room like you know you're hot, owning your sensuality, enjoying your appearance, or confidently expressing your attractiveness.

How it shows up
You second-guess putting on red lipstick, tone down your outfit if it might draw attention, or act goofy and awkward instead of letting yourself be sensual and magnetic.

2. The *Work Hard or You Don't Deserve It* Program

The spell in one line
This program says success only counts if it nearly kills you to earn it.

Validated for
Being constantly busy, working yourself to exhaustion, doing everything alone, visibly struggling, and earning approval through overwhelm and effort.

Judged for
Resting, receiving with ease, making money effortlessly, having success without struggle, or living a life that's pleasurable and flowing.

How it shows up
You jump off the couch to look busy when someone gets home, feel guilty taking a day off, make things harder than they need to be, or dismiss any success that felt easy as a fluke.

3. The *Don't Ask for Anything* Program

The spell in one line
This program teaches you that you need to be happy with what you're given and to not ask for what you want.

Validated for
Being quiet and patient, expressing gratitude for whatever you're given, avoiding requests, and suppressing personal preference or desire.

Judged for
Asking for anything, asking for more, asking for what you're owed, desiring extravagant, or claiming what you truly want — labelled greedy, selfish, or entitled.

How it shows up
You say *"Oh, I don't mind"* when you do, avoid asking for what you want for fear of seeming rude or selfish, try to get others to guess your needs, and feel hurt when they don't — because deep down, you believe you can't ask.

4. The *Don't Be Selfish* Program

The spell in one line
This program tells you that having your own desires, or prioritising yourself in any way, makes you selfish or bad.

Validated for
Putting others' needs before your own, always saying yes, being endlessly helpful, and sacrificing yourself in the name of being "good."

Judged for
Saying no, prioritising your own needs or pleasure, spending money on yourself, or choosing to make your life about what *you* want.

How it shows up
You find boundaries nearly impossible, say *yes* when you want to say *no*, and hide things you do for yourself for fear of being labelled self-centred.

5. The *You're Not <u>Allowed</u> to Be Powerful* Program

The spell in one line
This program tells you that it's not your place to be more powerful than others — e.g. earning more money than others (especially your parents) or positioning yourself as an expert.

Validated for
Deferring to others' opinions, doubting your own wisdom,

seeking guidance before acting, struggling visibly, and living according to what parents or society say is right.

Judged for
Trusting your own wisdom, doing something an authority in your life doesn't agree with, assuming a position of authority, or living in ways people you know wouldn't approve of.

How it shows up
You feel guilt or shame putting yourself out there as an expert, under-earn compared to your real capability, and feel uneasy about your pricing — like people will think you're charging (or earning) more than you should.

6. The *Don't Shine or Exceed Others* Program

The spell in one line
This program warns you that success = attack or rejection, so it's safer not to shine. If you shine, people won't like you.

Validated for
Blending in, exposing your flaws, being modest and humble, having similar struggles to everyone else, and never being *too* good at anything.

Judged for
Succeeding visibly, excelling beyond others, receiving recognition, shining too brightly, or being *too* confident in your brilliance.

How it shows up
You downplay or hide your success, sabotage yourself when things start going well, or rush to tell people what's been hard just to seem humble.

7. The *You Must Look Perfect* Program

The spell in one line
This program says that your worth lies in how beautiful, skinny, fit, hot, toned and perfect you look.

Validated for
Being effortlessly thin (but not *too* effortless), fitting beauty standards, having the "right" body type, having the "right" colour skin, and staying within the accepted spectrum of attractiveness.

Judged for
Aging, gaining weight, showing imperfections, not fitting beauty standards, or being beautiful *without effort*.

How it shows up
You hesitate to show up online if you don't look perfect, avoid the beach if you haven't shaved, or believe you need a "bikini body" to wear a bikini. You melt down over small weight fluctuations, believing you'd be more loved, successful, or respected if you just "fixed" your appearance.

8. The *Don't Seek Attention* Program

The spell in one line
This program tells you that wanting to be seen, or even be a star with fame and accolades in your industry, is shameful, self-absorbed, and wrong.

Validated for
Staying quiet unless invited to share, keeping your brilliance hidden, deflecting compliments, and pretending you don't want the spotlight.

Judged for
Wanting to be seen, claiming the spotlight, sharing your brilliance, or enjoying admiration — dismissed as attention-seeking or self-absorbed.

How it shows up
You avoid doing things that would draw attention, fear being seen as "too much" or "a show-off," and pretend you don't want to be seen — even though you secretly crave it.

9. The *Don't Think You're Special* Program

The spell in one line
This program tells you that you aren't special and have no unique significance — as if knowing your own brilliance is egotistical.

Validated for
Downplaying ambition, doubting yourself, self-deprecating, and acting like you don't think there's anything special about you.

Judged for
Confidence, ambition, knowing your greatness, or daring to believe you have something extraordinary to share.

How it shows up
You wait for outside validation — followers, approval, or proof — before sharing your brilliance. You downplay your ambitions, fear someone will say *"Who does she think she is?"*, and feel ashamed to admit what you really want.

10. The *Femininity Is Lesser* Program

The spell in one line
This program dismisses feminine energy, such as creativity, intuition, beauty, and spirituality, as frivolous, weak, or even unintelligent.

Validated for
Being logical, practical, and serious; prioritising intellect over emotion; valuing science, results, and productivity over intuition, creativity, or beauty.

Judged for
Expressing intuition, valuing beauty, honouring emotion,

embodying sensuality, or creating art and ritual — dismissed as frivolous, irrational, or naive.

How it shows up
You hide your spiritual side, second-guess your intuition, and secretly feel guilty or frivolous for loving beauty, ritual, or creativity — as if they make you less intelligent or grounded.

Now you understand what you've really been up against and why you kept finding yourself in loops of people-pleasing, playing small, and dimming your light despite your determination to live boldly.

It's not you — you've been under a spell.

A centuries-long illusion that dictates what's *acceptable* and what's *unacceptable* for a woman to be in this world.

Can you feel how much energy you'd liberate if you stopped trying to meet these standards and conform to these *illusory rules*?

Your *genius idea graveyard*? It's about to get a serious excavation.

Break the Spell — Reflection

- Which programs felt like a slap in the face?

- What were you told was *good* or *bad* in your childhood?

- How has your hidden rulebook shaped your life?

You don't have to live by this rulebook any longer.

The Good Girl Conditioning Spell may be centuries old, but we're the generation that breaks it.

Honestly? It's not even about just you anymore.

When you break this spell, you loosen the cultural grip of this toxic dogma that women now *keep themselves oppressed with*.

You show women everywhere — from daughters and nieces to friends, followers, and strangers passing you on the street — that they too can live for themselves, take up space, and shine.

When you break the spell for yourself, you break it for all of us.

Now, with all those illusory rules out of the way, it's time to look at what's been keeping you waiting...

Waiting to lead. To share your voice. To claim your authority. To unleash the full force of your energy, passion, and genius into the world.

Until you see this next spell, you'll keep mistaking your hesitation for truth — and you'll keep waiting.

SPELL THREE
Permission

The illusion that authority is crowned
— and why you're not stepping up.

SO MUCH OF MY WORK with women comes down to this — *permission*.

I don't mean giving it. I mean showing them they never needed it.

Remember that fear I told you about — the one where my mentor might read this book?

> *I keep getting stuck with this book because I'm afraid my mentor will read it and think it's both rubbish and flat out wrong, because I've presented my own ideas and not just shared exactly what I've been taught, as I was taught.*

This is my own permission wound. My wound against being an authority.

According to my ego, it's bad for me to have my own ideas — to present them as something of value and substance.

As if some authority needed to approve them first, to say: *Yep — you're allowed to say that.*

Women everywhere are unknowingly waiting for a blessing that doesn't exist — a silent nod to say they're allowed to own their ideas and be who they already are: *an authority.*

This sits inside *Good Girl Conditioning* — the part of the acceptable identity that says you're not allowed to crown yourself.

That's exactly why it deserves its own spotlight — because until you see it, it keeps you kneeling and waiting.

For centuries, a woman's authority has been conditional — granted by fathers, husbands, teachers, bosses, publishers, critics — everyone but themselves.

*The Permission Spell s*hows up as a feeling that a higher authority must recognise you first, and must anoint your idea as brilliant, worthy, and needed *before you dare to believe it yourself.*

Without it?

You're haunted by the poisonous thought… "*Who am I to?*"

- Who am I to start a fashion label?

- Who am I to sell my art for thousands of dollars?

- Who am I to put together a course as an expert? Do I have a fucking PhD or what? Have I published papers? *Am I a white male*?

- Who am I to sell premium experiences?

- Who am I to create my own method and then pitch it to corporations?

- Who am I to *write a fucking book*??

"Who am I to?" is the number one recruiter for the *genius idea graveyard*.

It's got the Ultra-Mega-Platinum position — it doesn't just have the Mercedes, it's got the whole factory. Top recruiter for 2,786 years straight.

Most little girls were taught, explicitly or implicitly: *You don't do anything without permission.*

You wait.

At school, you waited in line until the teacher said go. At home, you waited for mum's yes before you took the cookie. Your life quite literally ran on permission.

So you either followed that rule or did what you wanted — where no one could see. Not exactly a recipe for shining unapologetically.

Into your ego's little magical rule book to life it went: *You're not allowed until someone says you are.*

Wanna know something wild?

You're still doing this:

Still waiting before you own the power and importance of what you're here to share — only doing so once you've gained a certain amount of recognition.

I recently had a call with a coaching client of mine, Ambre, who, during her time participating in my mastermind, launched her own slow fashion brand.

Before joining the mastermind, she knew she wanted to launch this business, but she was completely stuck in, *who am I to?*

She had a vision to create this sustainable brand, designing and hand-making everything herself in France.

She had no qualifications to do this.

She hadn't studied fashion or design, or been trained to create patterns of any kind. And she'd never had a business.

What she had was a vision, and a burning passion to bring it to life.

She joined my mastermind because, although she knew this was what she wanted to do, she just couldn't get herself to start.

Once she'd joined, she started working on her first design — it needed to fit a wide range of body types, look stylish, make people feel amazing in their skin, and be made from upcycled fabrics.

Fast-forward eleven months, and she launched her product line with three unique designs she had crafted, immediately gaining customers and fans.

And then... the wildest thing happened.

In her very first month in business, a woman approached her to make a custom wedding dress out of upcycled fabrics and lace for her upcoming wedding.

That's right: Ambre, who had no prior experience and no formal qualifications saying she was "allowed" to do this — just a vision and passion, put her art into the world, and her genius was met with instant, raving fans.

So much so that, within her first three months in business, she had completed her first handmade wedding dress, with hand-dyed lace, all done by herself.

What the actual hell, right?

On a recent call with Ambre, I asked her what she'd learned from the whole process.

Here's what she said — and I want you to really hear it:

    1. *I can be a designer without going to fashion school.*

    2. *I'm so fucking skilful naturally, without training.*

    3. *Fuck the rules. The rules they teach in design school would have boxed me in. By not going, I invented my own pattern-making method that puts sustainability and*

creativity first.

4. *I can do what I want — this is my kingdom.*

She also said, *"I am over being acceptable."*

Before joining the mastermind, Ambre didn't believe she was actually allowed to do this. She was waiting for a permission slip she didn't need — and didn't exist.

She had to get out of her own way and let herself embrace her innate skill and talent because she'd been trained to believe she needed permission — some kind of tick of approval — to even have that skill.

Ambre's story is yours too — different details, same spell.

There's no permission slip coming to confirm you have a talent or that that talent meets some imaginary standard that allows you to offer it.

That concept is simply an illusion.

That was the spell all along. You've been waiting for a gatekeeper who doesn't exist.

Not for a book, a business, a method, a price point, a stage, a training, a painting, a line of skincare, a YouTube channel, a CEO client — or a wedding dress made from upcycled lace.

If you can envision it, you can claim it — at the full level you see it.

There never was any barrier in the first place.

If no one's ever looked at you and said, *"Who do you think you are?"* — you're playing too small.

It's time to stop waiting — and start being *unacceptable*.

Are you ready to make them say, *"Who does she think she is?"*

Break the Spell — Reflection

- What have you been unconsciously waiting for permission to do, own, or claim?

- What recognition, validation, or achievement have you assumed you need before taking things to the next level?

- What would you do this week if you stopped waiting?

Do you dare reclaim *that* from the graveyard?

Now, there's one more spell to break.

The one that's been convincing you that your deepest feminine traits — your sensitivity, sensuality, intuition, passion for beauty, emotion, and eros — are flaws to hide instead of powers to wield.

But when you reclaim them, everything changes — your energy, your magnetism, your ability to create and lead.

Ready to meet the parts of your power you've been taught to hide?

SPELL FOUR
Witch Wound

The illusion that your feminine nature makes you weak — when in truth, it's your greatest power.

WHAT IS THE *WITCH WOUND*?

I'm not talking about broomsticks or black cats.

I'm talking about the wound that taught women to fear their own feminine nature — their intuition, pleasure, eros, radiance, and connection to the divine.

Centuries ago, women who were wise, sensual, sovereign, and spiritually connected were burned for those very gifts. And somewhere in our DNA, the memory remains: It's not safe to embody our feminine nature.

That memory didn't just disappear — it evolved, mutating into the collective belief that those same feminine qualities aren't real strengths at all.

That intuition is *irrational*.

That sensitivity is *weak*.

That beauty, emotion, and eroticism are *frivolous* — or *dangerous*.

The Witch Wound is what lives on — the inner conditioning that makes women doubt the very qualities that once made them powerful.

To stay acceptable, most women suppress their feminine nature without even realising it — disconnecting, dissociating, and rejecting those qualities altogether.

They numb their pleasure, second-guess their intuition, brush off their creativity, and downplay their love of beauty — not because they want to, but because somewhere deep inside, the message still echoes: *It's not safe. It's not valid.*

But what exactly is this feminine nature we've exiled?

When I talk about *the feminine,* I'm not referring to gender — I'm speaking about the feminine *principle*: the receptive side of creation itself.

The sensual, magnetic, intuitive, emotional, and mystical part of you that perceives possibility and feels everything on every level — the energetic current that draws life and energy to you through your radiance.

This is what the *Witch Wound* taught women to suppress — their feminine essence. The very pulse that connects us to our power, creativity, aliveness, and magnetism.

This wound runs deep — and it shows up through four core expressions of the feminine that have been most distorted, silenced, or shamed.

Intuition. Spiritual Connection. Pleasure. Eros.

Each one is a doorway back to your full creative power, the essence of who you are, and connection to your life path. The part of you that *knows*, magnetises, leads, and lives turned on to life itself.

As we move through each, my intention is to help you see where you may have unconsciously shut down these gifts to stay acceptable — and how to reclaim them as the source of your radiance, magnetism, and natural power.

1. Intuition

Your intuition is your line of communication from your higher self. You can think of it like a radio station — a constant source of messages broadcast from your higher awareness, connected to all things across all time and space.

You can tune in to this "radio station" at any moment, about anything. The stream of information from your higher knowing is always there.

But that's not exactly affirmed by society, is it?

In our culture — at least in mine — intuition is treated as this slightly kooky thing you have to *admit* to believing in, because it's not inherently seen as real or valid.

When I was growing up, I didn't believe in intuition — or even that I had a soul. I'd been raised to believe only in what I could see, and anything unverified by science was fiction. If you believed in it, you were obviously an idiot.

Needless to say, I've grown a lot wiser.

We're not taught to trust ourselves or our inner knowing — in fact, we're taught *not* to. We're taught that someone else knows the way, someone else knows what's best for us.

I've been running courses on empowerment for many years now, and in almost every program I run, I get participants to complete an intake questionnaire. When I ask what women most want to get out of it, the top answers usually go something like this:

To trust myself.
To trust that I know what's right and best for me.
To trust my decisions.
To trust my inner voice.

Women are deeply wounded against their inner knowing — dismissed as "less intelligent" for using it as a source of guidance, as though logic and past experience were the only valid forms of information.

And to compound this judgement, no one ever taught you how to tap into that line of intelligence to effortlessly guide your life.

So no wonder you don't trust yourself to know what's best for you or make the right decision.

This has got to change.

One of the central things I teach in my work is intuition — because it's the only reliable source of truth. It is, in fact, our *higher intelligence.*

Everything else is filtered through the past: conditioning, fear, and the limitations of others.

Intuition, on the other hand, speaks from the now. It's connected to possibility, not programming.

Your intuition *is* your feminine nature in action — the unseen, higher intelligence the world taught you to distrust.

When you live from your intuition instead of your wounded ego, you stop looping in confusion, self-doubt, second-guessing, and giving away your power.

You pierce every one of these spells we've talked about — and start living from truth.

In my coaching, we use intuition for everything: to see your true life's vision, know your aligned next steps, uncover creations wanting to be birthed, and clearly see the exact fears, beliefs, and stories that are *really* holding you back.

It's the way out of the ego's maze — and into creation, freedom, and power.

Trust me when I say this: you can't think your way out of your ego. All you'll get is more confusion, more options, more overwhelm — and less clarity as to what you actually want.

Using your intuition to answer your questions and guide your life isn't just helpful — it *has to be* the source you live by.

Otherwise, you'll keep battling life from your wounds, and trying to make sense of your life through the lens of your ego's big, fat rule book.

I was fortunate to learn this essential skill from my mentor, William Whitecloud, who has a masterful way of teaching it.

We practice it through intuitive readings. People who've never tried it before — some who don't even "believe" in intuition — learn a simple process and then immediately give intuitive readings to people they've never met.

Every single time, they describe things about that person they couldn't possibly have known through logic or reason. And everyone is stunned — the reader, the person being read, everyone.

I've seen people cry because they felt more seen by a stranger over the internet than they ever have by their friends and family.

They say, *"What the actual fuck just happened? How is that possible?"*

It's possible because you're motherfucking connected to all things — through all time and space, boo. It's a natural ability that our culture has chosen to pretend it doesn't even exist.

This is the exact power women were once burned for — knowing what couldn't be proven, trusting what couldn't be seen.

Reclaiming your intuitive ability isn't just about making better decisions — it's about remembering the sacred line of communication between you and Source itself.

It's how your soul speaks to you, guiding you toward your highest path, your purpose, and the life you were born to live.

When you live life guided by your intuition, you become unacceptable to the systems that thrive on you following an external authority.

And that's exactly why it's so powerful.

2. Spiritual Connection

Most of the women I work with have gifts tied to their spiritual connection — yet one of the biggest hurdles I help them overcome is coming out of the *spiritual closet* and allowing that side of themselves to be seen.

I get it — I had to overcome it too. As a rational, maths-and-science-minded person, who identified strongly with intelligence and not being a "fool".

When I finally opened up to my spiritual connection, I projected that the world would see it as foolish too — even though I no longer did.

For years I tried to sound rational — to prove anything spiritual was rational and *legit.* But in trying to prove it, all I really did was go back to hiding it.

After my second money workshop in 2017, I realised this blockage wasn't helping anyone. In my marketing I avoided mentioning the spiritual elements central to my system, focusing only on the practical side.

As a result, I attracted people who didn't resonate — like one guy who only wanted to ask me about stocks the whole time. He didn't care about understanding his "money story" or deeper reason for creating financial abundance.

I also realised the people who would have loved my workshop weren't even signing up — because I was too afraid to admit what I was really about.

Lose, lose.

To come out of the spiritual closet, I had to get vulnerable to everything I feared might happen if I showed who I really was.

So the next workshop I ran, I claimed it.

And the women I attracted? Not only did they love it, they went on to work with me further, because my work resonated with them in a way no other approach to money ever had.

I'd be lying if I said that was the only breakthrough I needed.

I've had to catch myself sliding back into that closet many times — trying to prove, to sound logical, to make my spirituality *acceptable*.

Breaking a spell isn't about seeing through it once; it's about noticing when your ego lulls you back into hiding and deciding, again, to step out.

The more I said, *fuck it, I'm going to own it*, the more dream clients I attracted — women obsessed with my work, whom I was obsessed with serving.

And it's more than that — my work now goes far deeper and has far greater impact because I stopped pussy-footing around what I actually believe: that we have a soul, a purpose, and spiritual gifts to offer the world.

That we don't need to use our logical brains to figure anything out — we use intuition because that's how we know the truth.

None of that would be possible if I were still trying to make everything sound scientific and appeal only to the rational mind. Gosh, that would be hell.

People can only be drawn to your work, fall in love with it, *and* get the full benefit of it when you fully own who you are.

That's the way to access the unique gifts that make you stand out as one in eight billion.

It's time to come out of *the spiritual closet*.

When you stop hiding your spiritual nature, you gain access to the fullness of your gifts.

Your spiritual connection is part of your feminine nature — your connection to the Universe, the wisdom that feels and knows before proof.

When you allow it to flow through you, you don't just reclaim your spirituality — you reclaim the fullness of what you're here to offer the world.

This is what puts you on the podium — not strategy, not polish, but the courage to be authentic, even when it feels *unacceptable*.

3. Pleasure

Pleasure is one of the first things the good girl gives up.

Yet pleasure is one of the purest expressions of feminine energy.

Pleasure isn't just about sex, as most people think — we're so wounded around it. It's your embodied *yes* to life.

It's both a natural byproduct of being connected to your senses, and a portal into living in an open, receptive state.

Open to life.

Receiving life.

True pleasure isn't indulgence — it's the felt vibration of divine life-force flowing freely through you. It's your fully embodied feminine nature.

It's the experience of being in ecstatic union with life itself — and with your true desires.

Sound like a tall order?

This level of aliveness is available to you — you just never learned it was possible. Wild.

In my late teens and early twenties, I was completely shut down to pleasure.

And it wasn't because my body was "broken" (though at the time, I was convinced it was). It was because somewhere along the way, I decided it wasn't safe to be sexual or receptive to life.

So my (very intelligent) body shut it all down.

Because I didn't understand that, I felt completely fucked-up, broken, and like I was missing something everyone else had.

From the moment I realised something was off, I went looking for answers... and found nothing that explained it. Which only confirmed my fears that there must be something *seriously* defective about me.

For six years.

After six years of trawling the internet, seeing psychologists, and even doing a short stint on anti-depressants (because no one had any other ideas), I finally learned the thing that changed everything:

When your body doesn't feel safe to feel, it shuts "feeling" down — not because it's dysfunctional, but because it's protecting you.

I learned that this can come from all kinds of trauma — physical, yes, but also the trauma of growing up as a woman in a world where your body is treated as a target, and where you've constantly witnessed women being judged, shamed, and humiliated for being sexual.

And then I learned the best news of my life so far:

I could do something about it.

I could reawaken my natural orgasmic nature and my capacity for *insane* levels of pleasure — levels of pleasure and ecstasy I didn't even know existed.

When I finally heard it laid out like that, I thought: *How on Earth did it take me six years to find something this obvious? And why the hell doesn't the medical establishment seem to know this??*

So I went on a journey to reclaim what I had unconsciously disconnected from.

Very quickly I came face to face with how afraid and resistant I was to letting myself be *affected* by anything — even someone's touch.

It felt vulnerable. It felt like giving power away.

I had to dismantle the walls I'd built — not only against my sensual and sexual nature, but also against life itself.

I did week-long immersive retreats, explored all sorts of weird practices and rituals, saw bodyworkers, and even studied Somatic Sexology. I went down every avenue I could find to reconnect with pleasure — to let my body know, *it's safe to feel now*.

And I'm here to say — *I fucking cracked it.*

Oh my god. It took time. I even started to lose hope and reached points where I felt like I'd never get there. But I did. And I still think it's outrageous that what I eventually pieced together isn't common knowledge.

I went from being unable to feel any sexual pleasure at all, to opening into my full ecstatic nature and having every kind of orgasm — not just clitoral, but cervical orgasms, breast orgasms, energetic orgasms, even squirting orgasms (which, yes, every woman's body is capable of).

I can even move into an orgasmic state just by relaxing and breathing.

What I discovered blew my mind and changed my life forever.

I learned things about pleasure and sexual energy like:

- Pleasure is a natural byproduct of being open and receptive — it's far more expansive than sex alone.

- Pleasure is a portal to higher consciousness, creativity, intuition, beauty, and your unique essence.

- Pleasure regulates your body and nervous system, restoring calm, presence, and the knowing that all is well.

- Pleasure returns women to their radiance — their natural magnetism, balance, and life-force glow.

For most women, pleasure — and general openness and receptivity — is tangled up with pain, hang-ups, and fear. It was for me, too.

But any limitation a woman experiences around her pleasure is only because, somewhere in her psyche, she deemed it unsafe, invalid, or "too much". Not because she doesn't have a wild, innate capacity to be raptured by it.

Every woman's body holds the ability to experience earth-shattering pleasure — once the protective barriers are released.

Earlier this year I asked a group of women in a masterclass: *When are you allowed to feel pleasure?*

Their answers were heartbreakingly predictable:

After I've given first.
When I've earned it.
It's not allowed.
Never.

These aren't outliers — it's what I hear repeatedly.

Or, *Pleasure? That's not important.*

Beneath the surface, every woman I work with struggles to let herself *live* in her pleasure — to feel it daily, to create from it, to lead from it. It feels like she's not allowed. It feels like she's supposed to *switch it off* in order to live.

This is another thing I am unapologetically on a mission to change.

Pleasure is your birthright — the pulse of your feminine life-force. It's not some frivolous reward you *earn* after working hard enough, or some dangerous thing you shouldn't touch, as the spells handed down for generations would have you believe.

It's the byproduct of living wide open and in harmony with creation — the very thing that can fuel your creative power.

When you reclaim your pleasure, you break one of the oldest spells cast on women — the spell that says joy, beauty, and sensuality make you unsafe, unworthy, or useless.

They don't.

They make you magnetic.

Pleasure makes you creative. It connects you to intuition.

It is, in truth, *productive* to prioritise pleasure.

The world doesn't need more women cutting themselves off to remain rigid, unfeeling, and in control — it needs women lit up from the inside out, basking in their radiance, and creating from their pleasure.

4. Eros

Eros — the current of aliveness.

Eros is what pulses through your body when you let yourself be turned on by life itself.

It's not just about sex — it's the same *turned-on* current, but directed toward any creation: ideas, art, expression, leadership, purpose.

The tantrics call this your life-force energy; others call it creative energy — the energy at the source of creation.

It's that flood of aliveness you feel the moment inspiration hits, when seconds earlier you were half asleep on the couch.

Being connected to your eros amplifies every feminine ability — intuition, spiritual connection, pleasure — and grounds you in the unshakable *knowing* of who the fuck you are, exactly what you're here to do, and the total *rightness* of you doing it.

It's a portal into embodying your higher self — and feeling yourself as *her*.

When you live from this energy, everything becomes possible, passionate, and playful.

You become *unfuckwithable*. Undeniable. Magnetic — not because you're seeking attention, but because your presence commands it.

This is what the ancient practices of Sacred Sexuality have always known: Your eros is the gateway to your divine nature, your soul's blueprint.

I remember the first time I experienced this. I had been in the sacred sexuality world for a while. I'd cracked open my pleasure, but I hadn't yet had a *spiritual* experience through my sexual energy. Honestly, I thought the idea was romanticised — a little too dreamy for me.

But one day, something nudged me to revisit practices I'd learned years earlier when I was trying to awaken my pleasure.

No agenda, no expectations — just curiosity.

So there I was, on my green velvet couch, working with my energy — and suddenly, something opened.

Mid practice, I felt high.

Elated.

Jolted out of the anxiety I'd been drowning in, I was suddenly flooded with love — with the sheer beauty and bliss of being alive.

All I could do was cry tears of gratitude for life in this state of love and wholeness.

Things like "worthiness" stopped making sense. How could I possibly feel unworthy of doing the work I came here to do? It was laughable.

I suddenly felt an unshakable knowing of who I was, what I was here to share with women, and the absolute *rightness* of it.

All the usual head-fuck stories around my work, my viability and business dropped away. In their place was clarity — a simple divine desire that just felt true. And that? It was enough.

Leading up to this, I'd been fatigued for months, barely functioning. I was taking two-hour walks every day just to manage my anxiety.

And then suddenly — it was like being jolted awake. Energised. Plugged into Source itself.

Within days, I had organised a live event, booked it out, and by the end of that month, I'd doubled my income. It felt like a new dimension of life had opened.

What this shift opened up blew my mind.

So of course, I kept experimenting with these practices — learning their mechanics, discovering how it was they were working.

Eventually, I started teaching them in my existing programs.

And I watched the same thing happen to my clients: the same radiance, certainty, and creative power lighting up from within — and the same magical coming together of their lives and businesses.

Most of us were raised to believe sexual energy is only for intimacy or procreation. That was my assumption too.

My initial motivation for exploring pleasure was to "fix" my sex life. But what I found was infinitely deeper.

Sexual energy isn't just about sex — it's the source code of creation itself. *Your* source code.

It's a portal into higher states of consciousness.

Even Napoleon Hill knew this when he wrote *Think and Grow Rich* in 1937. He called sexual energy, when harnessed, the driving force behind human genius.

Is it any wonder then, that for thousands of years, religion and society have cast spells that made female sexuality dirty, sinful, and wrong?

Because a woman connected to her sexual power is a woman connected to her intuition, spiritual authority, and unshakable knowing of herself as divine. Not a recipe for subservience.

Through my work, I've watched woman after woman light the fuck up once they're connected to this energy — radiating the same certainty, bliss, beauty, and wild magnetism that flow when they're fuelled by eros.

It makes sense that eros has been made so profoundly unacceptable — reduced to the bedroom, confined to procreation.

No wonder so many women unconsciously shut down to it — unsure why they don't feel much, want much, or enjoy sex that much.

It's time to break the spell:

To remember that your divine feminine nature has nothing to do with wearing florals, baking, or gossiping — and everything to do with being erotically alive, deeply feeling, fiercely intuitive, and wildly magnetic.

A woman connected to this level of truth cannot be controlled, convinced, or contained.

She is a wild, untamable force connected to her essence.

Are you ready to come home to the power you've been sitting on all fucking along?

The truth is, babe — your feminine nature isn't weak.

It's raw, wild, and absolutely magnificent.

It's what makes you powerful. It's what makes you undeniable. It's what makes you unfuckwithable.

You've just been tricked into denying it to make you easier to control.

But we don't live in a time where you'll be burned at the stake for your power anymore.

We live in a time that's ripe for women to wake up from this spell — and reclaim their feminine.

The Witch Wound Spell ends with us.

Do this for all women, everywhere.

Break the Spell — Reflection

- How comfortable, open, and free do you feel in each of these four areas — intuition, spiritual connection, pleasure, and eros?

- Where do you notice the contraction or restriction?

- What raw, self-honest thoughts, feelings, or beliefs do you have about being *feminine*?

You've faced and revealed the core illusions that have kept you small.

Before I give you the Codes to break them, there's one more thing I want you to see — something that will show you how *not alone* you are, and how deeply *not personal* those convincing stories in your mind really are.

Seeing the Spells Speak

I RECENTLY ASKED THE WOMEN in my mastermind to write a list of everything their ego tells them they need to fix or resolve about themselves *before* they're allowed to go all in on their purpose — *before* they can have the business or success they truly desire.

To show you what the spells we've covered actually *sound like* in real life, I asked if I could share some of their lists here — unedited and in their own words.

These women are self-aware and trained to recognise these voices. They don't live by them. But as you've learned, the voices don't just disappear — they're still there, just relegated to the back seat.

I'm deeply grateful for these women's generosity in allowing me to share them with you. This is how we break the spells — together.

My intention in sharing them is simple: so you know you're not alone. We all carry these voices. You're not some special flavour of fucked-up — you're human. You've just been enchanted.

Read them and realise they're not personal — they're universal — and as such, they don't actually mean anything about you.

My list of things I believe are incomplete about me and I need to resolve before I fully go for my soul aligned business:

- *More solid or definite about exactly what I am offering i.e. I should be able to produce a polished 'elevator' pitch on demand.*

- *I need to have my Insta perfect, I need to be more polished, presentable, and perfect.*

- *I need to be in full health.*

- *I need to be more knowledgeable and 'trained'.*

- *I need to be fitter and toned and more beautiful and alluring.*

- *I need to have a 'theme' i.e. am I a zen woodland nymph or a noisy, edgy colour queen of give no fucks?*

- *I need to be credible, maybe even white.*

- *I need to have everything under control.*

My list of things I think are incomplete about me that I need to resolve before I can do the thing:

- *Having more art sales, so people can see that my work is in demand.*

- *Being successful in my business so people can trust that I know what I'm doing.*

- *Having more sales come through the gallery, so they can invest more in me. To show that I'm worthy of being in their roster of artists. To prove my legitimacy as an artist.*

- *Being more well-known and 'famous' in the art world.*

My list of incomplete things that I need to resolve before I go for my soul sustainable fashion business:

- *Being profitable and living from my craft (so contradictory).*

- *Having a Vogue-magazine-worthy house.*

- *Having amazing hair and nails (?!?)*

- *Coming up with an industry-recognised disruptive clothing pattern.*

- *Having thousands of followers.*

- *Mostly being successful to enable myself to be successful.*

- *Being distributed in exclusive concept stores.*

My list of what I think I need to resolve before I can do the thing:

- *I need to make the 'right' decision, that means overthinking everything so much so that I become overwhelmed and stuck in analysis paralysis, due to my fear of getting it wrong!*

- *I need to be confident and know what I'm talking about! That means studying and researching and buying another book or signing up to another free webinar or whatever... so I have all the information and know what I'm talking about.*

- *I need to have some money saved for a rainy day!*

- *It needs to be the right time of day with the perfect*

> *weather for the thing that I am doing! Sometimes even the right moon cycle and even zodiac sign so my energy is good, because I'm not allowed to be powerful on my own!*
>
> - *I need to try harder because everyone is better, smarter, skinnier, richer, more attractive, more intelligent, etc. than me and I don't get to have what others have.*

When you read these words, you're not just seeing other women's self-doubt — you're seeing our universal story of not being *enough*, not being *right*, or not being *allowed*.

Here's what I want you to remember — absolutely none of these statements are truth.

The story that says there are things we must fix, standards we must meet, boxes we must tick — then and *only then* will we be allowed to have what we want:

It's all a spell.

Every woman alive has her own version of this story running beneath the surface — even the most "together", successful ones.

The difference between the ones defined by it and the ones who are free?

The free ones wake up from the illusion.

So let's do that, shall we?

Part One Closing

You've seen the spells that bind you — the illusions that keep you small, safe, and acceptable.

You've felt the weight they carry. You've witnessed the pain they cause. And you've likely grieved what you feel has been lost because of them.

I won't deny — it can sting to face the truth. But the truth is what sets us free.

Without seeing it, you'd go on living under these spells — and what's meant for you *would* pass you by.

You *would* reach the end of your life wondering — *Was there more to life? Was there more to me that I never gave a chance?*

But now that you see the illusions you've been operating under, you have a choice — to live a different way.

The power to stop being seduced into a hypnotic state of obedience, and start claiming everything you were born for.

Are you ready to learn how?

In Part Two, I'm going to show you how to reclaim sovereignty over yourself and realign your life through six Codes that give you the power to break every spell you've been living under.

Let's continue into *The Divinely Wild Path of Being Unacceptable — The Codes That Wake You Up.*

PART TWO
The Divinely Wild Path of Being Unacceptable

The Codes that wake you up.

Introduction

IF PART ONE REVEALED THE spells that bind you, Part Two will teach you how to live beyond them — and walk the *Divinely Wild Path of Being Unacceptable*.

By now, you've seen that to get what you truly want in life, you must abandon the false sense of security that being *acceptable* gives you — throw out the ego's rule book, strip down (metaphorically), and *be unacceptable*.

Not unacceptable in truth — but unacceptable to your ego's idea of who you need to be.

To be unacceptable is to liberate yourself from the insidious belief that there's a *right* way to exist in order to earn happiness, success, or love.

That very preoccupation is the barrier between you and the effortless, unapologetic expression of your magic — the life you're truly meant to live.

Sounds great in theory.

But what we've also seen through these pages is that the *voice of acceptable* is seductive and convincing.

You've probably tried to step into your next level before, only to find yourself pulling back, getting distracted, or spiralling — despite the one million and one promises you've made that this time will be different.

As if some invisible force were holding you down — and not in a hot, kinky way, unfortunately.

That voice still has access to the control room.

So when overwhelm hits — or the fear of being banished for saying the wrong thing rises — you still find yourself frozen, unable to move forward. Even with the awareness of what's happening.

Because awareness alone isn't enough.

What do you actually *do* when you keep shrinking instead of shining — despite your best intentions?

Well, my dear, you have come to the right place. Because, that *is* my speciality and exactly what I'm here to unpack in the second part of this book.

Welcome to *Part Two: The Divinely Wild Path of Being Unacceptable*.

In the chapters ahead, you'll learn how to dismantle your mind's control tricks, reclaim your personal power, and embody the freedom that only the truly *unacceptable* ever taste.

INTRODUCTION

You have a path you were born to walk.

Let's get you on it.

CODE ONE

The Holy Hot Service of Self-Worship

Kneel at your new altar.

THE FIRST STEP IN EMBRACING your divinely wild, *unacceptable* nature is changing who you serve.

It's a sacred shift — from living in obedience to illusory rules, not to living in rebellion, *but to living in devotion to something else.*

Who's your daddy, boo?

In your *acceptable* orientation in life, you live to serve the expectations — real or imagined — of others.

Things like:

- how you should look,
- what you should say,
- what you should wear,
- who needs to approve your decisions,

- how ambitious it's "appropriate" to be,
- even which experts you're meant to quote before you dare speak your truth.

I could go on... but you get the picture.

What does the world think is valid?
What do my parents, partner, friends, or community think is valid?
And how can I live up to those expectations...?
Or not let anyone see that I'm not?!

You will never live the life you're meant for when *lining up for approval* is your daddy.

It's time to change masters.

Change masters to serving yourself — and no one else.

Sounds horrifyingly bad, doesn't it? *Licks lips.*
Positively scandalous. *Drums fingers together.*
Deliciously blasphemous. *Grinning with glee.*
A crime against the cult of conformity. Absolutely forbidden... *Howls at the moon.*

Which is exactly why it's the ultimate key to breaking the chains of being *acceptable*.

I'm not saying become selfish and only think of your own gain. In fact, what I am saying is a paradox.

Live to serve your heart's true calling — your 100% authentic self — and nothing else. Paradoxically, that's your highest service to the world.

That is what you have to choose.

This is a fundamental shift in what you make your life about.

Is your life about staying safe, maintaining approval, and getting everything "right"?

Or is your life about serving your soul's purpose?

It's one or the other.

There is no middle ground — the illusion of compromise only means you're still kneeling to the master of safety and approval.

If you truly want to create your most magnificent life — being unapologetically yourself — it's time to break that allegiance. It's the only way.

In 2020, I made a distinct shift in my coaching business — a natural result of changing my allegiance and embracing the *Holy Hot Service of Self-Worship*.

Before 2020, I was offering only money coaching.

I loved the work, but I knew there was so much more I wanted to share. Yet every business course I'd taken drilled in the same rule: pick one thing, master it, make money with it — *then* you can expand.

Do you hear it? The rules — the story that I have to meet certain "conditions" before I can do what I want.

So I followed what I believed were the rules of business — what the world would accept from me, and in what order.

My creative energy was like a shrivelled-up prune.

I loved money coaching, but I was holding myself back under the delusion that I couldn't yet offer the fullness of what I desired.

The more I obeyed that belief, the drier it got.

My business was rolling, but it was hard work and required every ounce of "push" I could muster. Financially, I hovered in a perpetual state of "just getting by".

Eventually, I burned out and I knew I had to make a change.

And to my great fortune, in 2020, the Melbourne lockdown brought my business crashing down — and what a wonderful doorway that opened.

With my main income source reduced to practically zero overnight, I took a part-time job that covered my baseline expenses. That meant I no longer needed my business to provide for me financially.

It was the best thing that could have happened.

It freed me from the desperate attachment to my business being my sugar daddy — the thing that had to support me — and from contorting myself and my work into whatever I thought would be liked, accepted, or trusted.

With that pressure gone, I asked myself:

Fuck it. If I put aside what I think people will pay for — what I think I have to do to make it work — what would I love to do?

If I didn't need it to "succeed", what would I love to create?

That night, I had a vision.

A monthly membership for women gathering to learn sacred sexuality practices — using pleasure, eros, and feminine embodiment to transform their relationship with money and purpose. And to connect with and support each other.

I felt the *trueness* of it through my whole body, and energy surged through me.

Then I realised — this was exactly what one of my clients had asked me to create after my first retreat earlier that year, where I'd guided them through a sex magic ritual one night.

I'd dismissed her idea at the time, assuming no one would pay me for something so outrageous, so "out there".

I told myself I needed to build a name first. I needed credibility. I needed success. I needed to *be someone* before I could pull off being so authentically me.

Or so I thought...

But with my newfound inner freedom?

I let myself imagine what I would *love* to offer — not loop in the head-fuckery of trying to predict what people wanted or would pay for.

Just: *what do I want to share with the world, without an agenda?*

As soon as I asked, I knew.

I would love to create this membership — and I knew it was exactly what these women wanted from me, too — the perfect example of that selfish/service paradox.

The next morning, I messaged ten women I thought might be interested. By the end of the week, I had seven women paid and enrolled.

I was ecstatic.

I ran that membership for two years.

Again and again, women told me how profound and transformative it was — how it gave them something they'd never found anywhere else.

One woman even credited manifesting her dream home — one that seemed utterly impossible — in large part to these practices.

For many, it was the first time sexuality clicked as a pathway to empowerment and creation. They said:

"This was the missing piece — the exact "how" to move, direct, and embody sexual energy to connect with my higher self and creativity. The thing other sexuality teachers talk about but never show."

If I'd kept serving my idea of acceptable, I would've robbed those women of transformation.

After that, I let myself create whatever courses I fucking wanted — whatever felt true and alive in my heart and body, I made that. And I was on fire.

Before long, my business crossed the holy six-figure milestone, and I had everything I needed to move to Bali.

This didn't happen because I nailed my "one message," or mastered my marketing, or figured out how to speak to "people with money", or got noticed by someone famous.

Nope.

None of that.

It was because I changed my master — and that changes everything.

No longer serving the voice of acceptable in my head, I devoted myself to the *Holy Hot Service of Self-Worship* — radically and unapologetically living to serve my soul's calling, without validation or guarantees.

I offered what I fucking wanted to offer the world, how I wanted to offer it — showing up as outrageously, unacceptably, authentically me.

My life changed because of that.

My business' collapse was the best thing that ever happened to me.

It brought me to my knees — and to my true altar:

My heart. My soul. My Greatness. My calling.

This is my invitation to you, too — *change your master.*

Embrace *The Holy Hot Service of Self-Worship* — the real selfless act.

This is the turning point — the moment you claim your path back. And with it, everything the world wants to give back to you.

None of the Codes following mean anything without this foundation.

You're either ready to switch or you're not.

Will you choose it?

Are you ready to kneel at your new altar?

Initiate This Code: Swear Your Devotion

Alright, boo — it's time to kneel at your new altar. Grab a pen and paper, open your heart, and get ready to write.

Step 1: Name your master
Title your first page: *The Approval Daddy.*

List every rule you've been unconsciously trying to obey and every invisible standard you've been measuring yourself against.

Ask yourself:

- *What do I still think I have to fix about myself?*

- *Who am I trying to prove myself to, or not upset?*

- *How am I trying to be respectable, safe, or valid?*

Step 2: Crown your true authority
On a new page, title it: *My Soul's Calling.*

Now imagine your every need taken care of. You're whole, complete, and fully taken care of by life. You're sorted, boo.

From that place, ask:

- *What do I love?*

- *What matters to me?*

- *What lights me up and sets my heart on fire?*

Pick up your pen and write, without stopping, for ten minutes. Don't edit. Don't think. Let it pour through you. Imagine, dream, make it up — and just write.

Step 3: Devotion
What you just wrote are the threads of your true essence — your *new* authority.

Write one sentence that begins: *"From this day forward, I serve..."*
and finish it with your own words — a vow to your higher nature and purpose.

Say it out loud. Feel it in your heart. Kneel at that altar.

❖ **Dive Deeper on the Podcast**

There's a fundamental question that not many people ask themselves: *What are you making your life about?* This question changes everything. What are you kneeling to? Listen to the following episode to unpack this Code further and *see exactly what you've been making your life about* — and how to choose, consciously... security or heart, pleasing others or self-worship.

*Episode 152: What are you making your life about — from the **Money, Sex, Business & Awakening Podcast**.*

Listen here: *beunacceptablebook.com/podcast-152*

Congratulations, boo.

You've taken the first — and most fundamental — step on the *Divinely Wild Path of Being Unacceptable.*

But I'm going to be real with you, because most people won't — and that's why you've been stuck: None of this is a one-time spell break — it's a daily devotion.

Stop working out? Your muscles atrophy.

Stop committing your allegiance each day, each moment, each decision? Your default programming, set in stone by your ego all those years ago, creeps back in. And before you know it, you're living to please and appease again.

You've just drawn the line in the sand — now you must devote yourself to it.

Every fear, every doubt, every urge to shrink and run back to the sweet, sweet sugar high of approval — remember which altar you kneel at now.

With that in place... let's get you taking action with Code Two.

CODE TWO
Feel Unworthy & Do It Anyway

Bless, then banish your bullshit.

REMEMBER HOW I SAID THAT the *gaping hole of incompleteness* is an inherent part of your ego, and it's not going anywhere?

Yep. *It's not going anywhere.*

You will feel it forever! *Mwahahahaha.*

But it's not so bad — there are things we can do to make it less painful and stop it from running your life.

This is where you've gotta start being willing to face and feel your scariest demons.

You know what gives those demons power?

Two things.

> 1. You *believe* them.
>
> 2. You *resist* them.

That terrible, sick feeling that screams *you're not okay and it's not going to be okay?*

That's your ego flagging an old threat from childhood — not a true reflection of what's happening right now.

It's a projection from the past, not a fact about the present.

The gaping hole hijacks your control room the moment you believe that projection and act on it.

The story it tells you produces an emotion, even if that's numbness, and that emotion compels you to do something...

Things like:

- Don't share the post you just wrote.

- Don't send that pitch — scroll instead.

- Leave [important thing] for later and eat some cake.

- Delay launching your course and sign up for another training instead.

- Stalk what others are posting to decide what you should post.

- Stop to "rest" under the guise of self-care — when really you're avoiding the fear, self-doubt, and the follow-through action that would actually relieve the stress.

No, babe. We're not doing that anymore. That way of life is over.

When you obey what the gaping hole is compelling you to do, you give it the controls. That's *how* it gets its hands on them and takes over your life.

But we're here to take the controls back.

So here's what to do instead when your survival brain floods you with emotion and screams there's something wrong, you're not okay, and you shouldn't do the thing:

Here's the Code: *Feel Unworthy and Do It Anyway.*

This phrase came to me in 2021 and has become a mantra I share ever since.

You can replace *unworthy* with any flavour your gaping hole is serving — *not enough, incapable, wrong, not allowed, bad.*

Feel that — and do it anyway.

Feeling unworthy, undeserving, or not ready is not a reason to stop. It's a false signal coming from your ego's spells.

Want to pitch a store to stock your product, but feel embarrassed and ashamed because you're "a nobody"?

Feel Unworthy and Do It Anyway.

Want to share what you really think online, but you're afraid people will judge or disagree?

Feel Unworthy and Do It Anyway.

Want to show up on your stories, but fear they'll think, *She's not successful or important — who does she think she is?*

Feel Unworthy and Do It Anyway.

That's the path — not to achieving perfection, but to following truth.

It's how you create what you're meant to create, and how success finds you naturally — because it's what you were born to do.

A woman in my mastermind a few years ago came to me wanting to grow her coaching business and replace the income she earned in her previous employment. Let's call her Sally.

Sally dreamed of working 1:1 with women in leadership, helping them unlock their desires and step into full power — but she didn't believe she was *allowed* to build a high-end, intimate offer yet.

She believed she was too early in business and had to follow certain steps before she dared offer something so high-priced, so high-promise, and such a long-term commitment.

After all, she'd never sold high-ticket coaching, never even sold a bundle of coaching sessions, and only had a handful of clients.

Those god damn business courses.

The first thing I did was help her identify what she actually wanted to do — because actually, she hadn't even admitted to herself yet that this was what she wanted.

Once she admitted she didn't actually want to run group courses, which she thought she had to in order to build her business, we looked at the story she was telling herself about why she couldn't go for what she wanted yet, and what she had to do instead.

My advice after that? *Feel Unworthy and Do It Anyway.*

And being the courageous, committed woman she was, she did.

Shaking, she pitched a dream client — 12 months of 1:1 coaching for $10k.

Totally unacceptable by everything she'd been taught.

Her brain screamed — *you're not qualified, not experienced enough, not credible yet.*

The client's response? A full *fuck yes*.

And not just a fuck yes — she was *grateful* for the offer. It was exactly what she'd been craving.

Remember the paradox? Serving what you love is your highest service to the world.

If my client had obeyed the "unworthy" feeling, she'd still be playing small.

Not offering her full wisdom to the people that wanted and needed it...
Not making the money she could have...
Not making the impact in people's lives she could have...

All because of an unquestioned assumption that feeling unworthy actually means something.

Instead?

She chose to stop going along with the charade and wake up to the truth:

There are no rules. You can do what you want. You can have it. And when it comes from your heart — it is *service*.

The result?

She built her business the way she wanted, served her clients at a much higher level, and soon replaced the income from her previous job.

You don't need to feel ready, worthy, or good enough.

You just need to apply this Code and remember:

Worthiness is a feeling, not a fact.

You're meant to feel unworthy — and do it anyway.

Initiate This Code: Fuck What You Feel, Choose to Serve

It's time to burn the belief that worthiness exists. You act because sharing your gifts is a *holy hot service* — not because you feel wanted by the world or think you're good enough to do the thing.

Step 1: See the story
Think of something you *know* you want to step into or claim in your life — a step into your Greatness. Something that feels edgy. Like: *"Holy fuck, I would die so happy if I did/ became that!"*

Now, answer these questions:

- *What are you telling yourself you're lacking or missing right now to be able to do it?*

- *What do you believe you need to fix, change, or resolve so you can do or be this?*

Step 2: Dissolve the projection
Now, imagine none of those things you wrote down are true or real. Literally — imagine they're illusions of your imagination.

If that were the case, *what would you do?*

Step 3: Act on your vision
Now imagine that it is your sacred duty — your *Holy Hot Service*

to the world — to take the action from Step Two. Your divine assignment, if you will.

Feel unworthy.

Do it anyway.

> ❖ **Dive Deeper on the Podcast**
> If you want to understand not only *why* your dreams stir up feelings of unworthiness — but also how that discomfort is actually part of the process — listen to the podcast episode below.
>
> *Episode 117: Your dreams will always make you feel like shit — from the* **Money, Sex, Business & Awakening Podcast.**
>
> **Listen here:** *beunacceptablebook.com/podcast-117*

You don't need to heal your unworthiness before you act.

In fact, you don't need to heal it, *ever*.

Feel the fear. The doubt. The *I'm not good enough*. The *they'll all hate me*. The *what am I even doing, of course they'll say no, I'm going to look like a loser*. And do it anyway.

This is true power.

It's not about feeling good all the time or never having a negative thought — it's about facing the fire of your illusion and choosing your potential over your projection.

We're no longer in the land of fluffy, feel-good manifestation — the one that sells you the fantasy that if you're "doing it right", everything should be glitter and rainbows. The one that has you repeating affirmations and stuffing down every negative emotion that arises, meanwhile feeling more and more powerless, because those emotions seem to prove you haven't got it right yet. So you hide them too.

No. Ew.

This is true spiritual realisation — and real power to shape your reality.

These Codes are the portal to your wild, creative, thoroughly alive, magnificent life — the one you were born for.

And the only way through that portal is through the fire — through feeling the intense, uncomfortable emotions you've been taught to interpret as something wrong.

To be powerful you don't need to stop feeling them. You need to *Feel Unworthy and Do It Anyway*.

Write on a sticky note.
Set it as a reminder.
Put it on the fridge door.
Tattoo it on your face — whatever it takes to remember this Code.

Where you once saw barriers and long timelines, suddenly there are none — because there's nothing you need to secure first. You just do it.

Now, I know it doesn't always feel possible to simply act when you feel stuck in your shit storm — and if that's exactly what's crossing your mind right now, I got you. That's exactly why Code Three exists.

Next, you're going to learn how to take your power back from the *feels* that make you freeze — and it might just be one of the most important things you ever learn.

CODE THREE
Celebrate How Gloriously Wrong You Are

This is self-love.

WHEN THE FEELING OF UNWORTHINESS grips you by the throat and won't let go ...

You *want* to act.

You *want* to move forward.

But you feel choked. Trapped in a swirling fog of pain, self-pity, and powerlessness.

Yes, I know about it.

No, I haven't been watching you — I have the same experience — and so does almost every other woman.

I'm about to give you another tool that feels absolutely outrageously simple, yet will melt you out of that very freeze and debilitating funk in a matter of *seconds*.

Yes, seconds.

A funk that you might have lost yourself spiralling in for days, weeks, months, or even *years*.

Trust me, I know. Even as a trained coach, with a coach myself (but we'll get to that story in a moment).

This tool is called, *Celebrate How Gloriously Wrong You Are*.

Because you, my love, will *feel* wrong — deeply, gut-twistingly wrong. So wrong, you'll wish you could melt out of existence — even when you're on the exact right path, doing brilliant things.

You will, at times, feel like you're getting everything wrong, doing everything wrong, or the very essence of you is wrong.

Any of the following sound familiar?

You're going to buy something, so you pull out your phone and look at your bank balance. Suddenly, you feel sick — the number staring back at you reminds you that you don't have your shit together, and how powerless you feel about it.

Omg, I'm not okay, why can't I figure this out — wtf is wrong with me?

You're excited to run a masterclass. You write up a description, set up registrations, and start shouting about it online — convinced, everyone will want to join! You then proceed to refresh your email every 15 minutes to check registrations. The end of the day comes, and still no one has signed up. Suddenly, you feel sick.

Omg, why hasn't anyone signed up — wtf is wrong with me?

You're pumped to make a video on a topic you love. You get out your phone and hit record. The words don't come out right. You sound tangled, unconvincing — like an idiot. Fifteen takes later all you want to do is cry and give up on ever creating videos.

Omg, I thought I had something interesting and important to share — wtf is wrong with me?

Let's get one thing straight — you are not *wrong*.

Nothing about you is wrong.

And — your soul never feels *wrong*. Your soul feels *truth*. It feels what's alive, or not. It feels *resonance*.

Feeling wrong?

That's the world of your ego and its big fat motherfucking rule book — the claws of the gaping hole and Good Girl programming trying to drag you back into your cage.

So then, what do we do about this gripping feeling of fucked-up-ness when it descends, threatening to pull you into a spiral?

We celebrate it.

Sayyyy what???

You heard me! *We. Celebrate. It.*

And it's glorious.

I first learned this profoundly simple alchemical hack from Carolyn Elliot's work in *Existential Kink*, and if you want to explore it more deeply, I recommend reading the book.

It's deceptively simple but not necessarily easy when you get started. Once you get the hang of it though — it works in seconds.

Here's the thing about your ego, it will fight tooth and nail to try and make the horrible feeling of wrongness go the fuck away — which unfortunately, only reinforces it. Because the need to get rid of it feels so strong, you become terrified of this feeling and convinced that you absolutely must reject it.

But the opposite is true — and that's the practice here.

Once you surrender to the feeling instead of fighting it? You unlock an entirely new level of creative power.

Let me show you how it helped me rise above and resolve one of my most stubborn battlegrounds — emotional eating. It ain't pretty, but it's definitely relatable.

I've had an on-again, off-again dysfunctional relationship with food, and by extension, my body and health.

Recently, for the first time in ten years, I was completely, and mercilessly dominated by it again.

I thought I had "healed" it. I thought I was over it. I thought I'd reached a level of self-love with my body that it couldn't possibly happen again.

How very wrong, and very, very humbled I was.

Near the end of an overseas trip, it hit me in full swing.

Daily anxiety about food, compulsive eating habits I had no control over, the feeling of hunger that wasn't hunger, not being able to tell what was compulsive and what was reasonable, gaining weight, feeling disgusting, intense shame, and absolutely gripped by an obsession to fix the whole thing — *yesterday* — and get back to normal.

Do you relate to this kind of experience in any area of your life?

Naturally, because I felt so damn awful and wrong, I was trying everything I could think of to shift out of the pattern and the raging storm of self-rejection happening in my mind.

But nothing worked. No process. No coaching session. No looking in the mirror and trying to love myself. Nothing.

I was hovering between 6-8kg heavier than usual, and I was bloated approximately 100% of the time.

To compound things, each day, by midday, the lower half of my body would swell up like a balloon with fluid and I'd look, feel, and *be* even bigger.

The real problem wasn't really the weight gain — the real problem was how it triggered me to feel so *wrong*.

The unconscious story my ego was projecting onto my circumstances was this:

My body doesn't work properly, I don't work properly, I have no power and control over myself — and therefore I have no power or control over my life. I'm simply defective.

I desperately wanted to make it go away and feel good about myself again — to banish the absolute and utter wrongness I was feeling. But all that did was keep me locked in it.

I was even trying to feel neutral about it, but I couldn't get my brain to unhook for long. Before I knew it, the obsessive thoughts about how I could make it stop would start looping again.

Fortunately, it was during this time that I finally read *Existential Kink* — which had been on my reading list for four years — and I saw exactly how I was continuing to fuck myself.

I was attempting to take my energy out of the problem and redirect it into my true vision, but my focus remained locked on the problem because I was in *so* much resistance to it.

And nothing I was doing was making any meaningful progress in melting the iceberg of that resistance.

Inspired by Carolyn, I applied my newfound insight.

What if, every time I catch myself in the mirror and feel that sense of disgust seeing my body, or every time I feel that intense anxiety that makes me want to eat, or every time I feel powerless, broken, and out of control — I celebrate it?

I welcome it.
I embrace it.
I invite it.
— I even go beyond just those things and throw a 60-second part-aaay for it.

Hell, it was worth a shot!

It was scary to do because my ego was committed to the idea that I must *not* be any of the things I was feeling; disgusting, fat, ugly, out of control, powerless, or imperfect.

But I got brave and did it anyway.

When I saw myself in the mirror, my heart would drop and the sickening feeling of disgust would hit me. But instead of letting myself shut down in that moment, as I usually did — I stopped and switched to celebrating it instead.

I know, it sounds crazy and deranged. It's taking a total 180 on the situation.

Like a cray cray cheerleader, I'd put it on thick and start raving with full goofy enthusiasm:

"*Yes, I feel so disgusting! Yes! Yes! Yes! I'm such a big pile of disgusting shit. Yes! Omg. Yessss. I'm so ugly. So gross. So disgusting. Yes, guuuuuurl. Get it!!!*"

Then I would burst into laughter. And wow — it felt good.

The result?

The constant head-fuck, obsession, and soul-crushing inner turmoil I was experiencing about "my problem" started to *melt away*.

Not only did the exercise make me laugh, it snapped me out of descending into the story and the gripping feeling that something was terribly wrong with me — as if out of a trance.

And then? I'd simply get on with my day.

As this fog cleared, the very obvious solutions and next steps to lose the weight and have a healthy relationship with food again suddenly revealed themselves — things that had been there all along.

Why? Because I was no longer buried under the weight — and delusion — of feeling broken and powerless. I could see clearly again.

So I acted on these obvious steps.

And what do you know, boo — I regained my power.

Holy shit, finally.

After almost eighteen months of flailing around like a wet fish in a bucket, crying that nothing worked and it wasn't my fault I was fat, my body was broken, it wasn't *me* — I finally stopped feeling like, and *being*, a victim. I took my power back.

I lost the extra weight *(turns out, not that hard)*, and even resolved 90% of the bloating in the process. I returned to an even fitter, hotter, healthier version of myself.

Now, I'm not saying there wasn't other inner work involved — but applying this Code created the shift that cracked everything open for me to see how I, in fact, did have the power.

It allowed me to authentically step out of my story and see the path forward to what I really wanted — and to act on it. A pathway that had been there all along, but had been hidden beneath resistance and self-judgment.

All because I embraced every part of how wrong and fucked up I felt.

And not only that, I celebrated it, turning myself back on and opening myself back up to life.

By doing so, I let myself return to knowing that all is divine.

Here's what really landed for me after going through that experience:

When you reject or resist anything about yourself — when you feel that something about you or your life needs to change *immediately* for you to be okay (for me, that was losing weight and not emotionally eating) — you move into a state of separation.

You disconnect from your wholeness, and in doing so, from your higher self.

From that point, your ego takes the wheel. You slip into a dysfunctional state where you *can't see* the obvious path your higher self is leading you toward — the one aligned with your true, healthy, abundant existence — because you've separated yourself from it by believing there's something wrong.

As long as you feel bad about *feeling bad*, you stay invested in your sense of separation from what you want and you experience yourself as separate from it — keeping you looping in your story, unable to break out.

But your soul?

Your soul knows that you are whole and complete as you are right now.

It approves of *everything*. It lets *everything* exist.

Nothing is wrong or bad. There is simply what's *preferred* and *aligned* — and that's what it's constantly guiding you toward.

That means there's also nothing wrong with you for being out of alignment in any way. It's all okay. You're okay.

When you celebrate *everything* — even the parts your ego wants to exile — you reconnect with that wholeness. You plug back into your higher self.

That's why celebrating what your ego rejects is such a powerful way to return to your sense of wholeness.

It dissolves the illusion that there is anything truly wrong, and in that moment, your energy is freed — freed to flow toward your truth, rather than locked in resistance to your fear.

This is radical approval — for every part of yourself and every part of your life, *right now.*

Not when you're making more money.
Not when you've lost weight.
Not when you have more ducks in a row.
Not when you have more attention.
Not when you've nailed everything perfectly.

Now.

Radical approval is the gateway back to your soul. Radical approval of *everything* — including all those yucky, sticky parts of you that you think are the most grotesque things ever... so horrible and wrong that you must hide or get rid of all costs.

At this point the biggest resistance I encounter when I teach this is, *"But Alex, if I accept this, won't I stay stuck here? I need to stay unhappy with it and reject it, so I do something about it — I don't want to stay here!"*

When you stop fighting what you hate, you take your energy *out* of it. And suddenly, you can see your soul's next move toward alignment.

That's the truth of it. Approving, loving, welcoming, and celebrating are not resigning. This practice is enabling yourself to come into the truth of your wholeness, into connection with your higher self, and act in the most functional and empowering way.

This is the *real spiritual work*.

This is true liberation.

Not fucking vision boards.

Not chanting *"I am a wildly wealthy woman"* in the mirror ten times before you leave the house in the morning.

And definitely not pretending you don't have a team of demons whispering nightmares in your ear when you feel most vulnerable.

No.

It's facing the gripping freeze head-on — even when you feel like you might die — and then feeling it soften and your heart melt open again, as you wake yourself up from the illusion that you were ever not whole.

This is how and when you remember that nothing was ever wrong.

You're magnificent. Glorious. Powerful beyond comprehension.

But you only *experience* that truth when you embrace yourself as that — by celebrating every single part of you, whether it feels like the most fucked-up thing ever, or the most wonderful and brilliant.

I've now taught this deceptively simple practice to countless clients, and every single one has said the same thing: It shifts their energy in seconds — from anxiety, shutdown, and fear to open, flowing, and un-fucking-bothered.

Celebrating How Gloriously Wrong You Are is a spiritual portal — a way back to your higher self, and to living the life you're meant for.

Because in that moment, you reconnect to your divinity.

Initiate This Code: It's Hot Kinky Celebration Time

You're not leaving this chapter without giving this deliciously weird practice a try. It's time to embrace every single part of you in love — so let's go there.

Step 1: Go there

Bring to mind the most triggering situation you're facing right now — the one that makes you feel bad, wrong, fucked-up, or incomplete.

Write it down.

Step 2: Name your wrongness

What story is your ego telling you about what this means about *you*? And what do you absolutely *not* want to be but *feel like* you are because of this condition? (e.g., incapable, a failure, disgusting, selfish, a loser, etc.)

Step 3: Get willing

Are you willing to let yourself embrace being "that"? You don't have to like it, but just for the next five minutes, imagine putting down the fight against it and embracing it, exactly as it is.

Say to yourself, *"I am willing to own and embrace being X"*.

Step 4: Celebrate how gloriously wrong you are
If you can let it exist and embrace it (even just for five minutes), then it's time to take it a step further and celebrate it!

In your mind's eye, imagine throwing it a goofy ass party. Cheer it on. Tell it to *go get it girl! Right on! You slay baby.* Be over the top. Dance with it. Laugh with it. Be ridiculous.

Go there. Keep going there.
And just... *watch what happens.*

❖ Dive Deeper on the Podcast

If you're ready to take this topic ten levels deeper, join me for this podcast episode to not only explore celebrating what's so wrong with you, but also uncover exactly why you're creating this super unwanted thing in your life... Because the next level truth? It's that some part of you is getting *exactly what it wants*. When you uncover what that is, even more power opens up for you to change it.

*Episode 126: Shadow integration - realising your unconscious kinky desires — from the **Money, Sex, Business & Awakening Podcast**.*

Listen here: *beunacceptablebook.com/podcast-126*

Wow, babe — I have to say, I am *so proud* of you for getting here.

Maybe when you picked up this book, you thought it was going to be another cute, kitchy, feel-good *empowerment* book — you know, a bit of sparkle and affirmation.

"*You can do it! Just believe you can. Here's an affirmation for your mirror.*"

Vom.

But instead you got the gut wrenching *real spiritual work*. Sorry-not-sorry.

Not everyone's willing to go there. Most people want to stick to the shiny looking path and pretend their shit don't stink because it's too confronting for them to see what's really going on.

But not you — not if you've made it this far anyway. So I see you, and I'm celebrating you. You kinky-ass babe, you.

And if you're still struggling to celebrate your glorious wrongness, that's okay too.

Don't stress about it, and don't make that another thing to feel wrong about! It's a practice — one that asks you to die to everything your ego says will kill you. So, it's understandable that it can take some work to fully drop into.

You have what it takes though, I know you do. Just keep intending to get there with it, keep applying the other Codes, and it will come.

Now we've got your energy moving and flowing — in the next Code I'm going to show you how to claim your crown and take the fucking throne you're meant to be sitting on.

Let's go.

CODE FOUR

You Are the Permission You've Been Waiting For

You're the daddy now.

THERE IS NO MAGICAL AUTHORITY in the world that you need permission from to do what you would most love to do.

Obviously, if you're going to do brain surgery or argue in court, you need skill and training — I'm not denying that.

But the days of needing mummy and daddy's permission to do something are over. Your ego just hasn't realised yet.

You're the daddy now.

If you want to start selling handmade clothes out of upcycled jeans and bed sheets — you can do it.

If you want to build a cult-like following by making Egyptian-style custom gold jewellery — you can do it.

If you want to publish a book of drawings illustrating the human journey of self-discovery — you can do it.

If you want to guide others to living a better life through any means that turns you on — you can do that, too.

Whatever's in your heart, you can do it. The fact that it's in your heart *is* your permission.

And what I listed above aren't hypotheticals — these are all things my clients have claimed for themselves and are doing *right now*.

You have the power to give yourself the permission you've been *waiting f*or — simply by deciding it gets to be yours.

You are the permission you've been waiting for.

Once that truth really lands? The ceiling on how big you let yourself be comes off.

Let me show you.

I recently took part in a sales challenge. Each day, we were given a prompt to create a piece of content on.

Most of the prompts focused on showing your ideal clients that you understood the problem they were experiencing, and how to solve it.

However, there were a few unusual prompts mixed in...

On day twenty I opened the prompt, and what I read made my heart rate go up.

I thought, *Are you for real? You want me to say that??*

The prompt was;

"How I'm Taking Over the X Industry in [year]" — for example, "How I'm Taking Over the Pet Sitting Industry in 2025".

The audacity! *Scoffs*.

My immediate thoughts were;

How could I make a claim like that? I don't have that kind of authority. I'm not allowed to just declare I'm taking over an industry when, on the global scale of my industry, I'm a nobody.

Wow.

Talk about revealing where I believed I didn't have permission to go.

One look at that prompt, and I realised I had an unconscious assumption that before I could make a claim like that, my work needed to be validated by mass adoration and obsession.

In other words, my ego had determined that before *I* could believe my work had a big contribution to make to my industry, it needed to be validated by others — and not just a handful of people — it had to be the masses. Probably including a publishing deal that a huge publishing house *reached out to me* for.

Then I could *act like an industry leader*. But not before.

It was an incredibly illuminating moment.

Of course, I took up the challenge that made me feel so uncomfortable — and here's what I wrote from my heart;

How I'm taking over the personal development industry in 2025

1. No more 'fixing' - you're fucking whole/ healed and a genius as you are. You just need to learn how to switch into that mode in your consciousness.

2. Working your mind, emotions & eros TOGETHER to unhook from fear & embody your full power, passion & high vibrational state.

3. Shadow work that doesn't just gloss over the surface — it takes you to the scariest corners of your consciousness and drenches those places in "turn-on", liberating your energy so your shadow no longer owns & sabotages you.

4. Getting so down and dirty with your fear that you can transmute it into hot, hot turn-on in a matter of minutes.

5. Turning on your eros, magnetism & feminine energy so that you can attract like a mf & create from your highest frequency energy... overflowing ideas & clear intuition at your fingertips all day, every day.

6. Training you to be completely unconditional in your creating - no timelines, no conditions, no limitations... tapping into the true possibility and potential around you.

7. Creating from TURN-ON.

It's gonna be LIT.

This is the new Self-Mastery for women.

Made by a woman. Made to work for women.

Who's ready??

And then I vommed in my mouth slightly as I posted it.

The result?

Something shifted in me.

Yes, that is what I'm doing.

That's what I'm about.

What I wrote in that post *are* the things I find so important and essential for women to achieve transformation and power in their lives — that I don't see anywhere else.

What I wrote *is* the body of work I've built over these years.

It's all the things that I've found to be the difference between women (myself included) staying stuck in "working on themselves" and not really making real leaps in their life, and women creating the lives and businesses that set their hearts and souls on fire.

I've seen these unique things that I bring to the industry unlock everything women were never able to before — even after years of the personal development merry-go-round, doing every spiritual *butt-hole activation* under the sun.

I've watched my existing clients hit entirely new levels once I began integrating my unique approach and the tools I've developed to practice it.

I was having a light bulb moment after writing this post...

This is how I'm here to disrupt the industry — by restoring women to their innate power to live free, turned-on, hot AF lives, sharing their magic with the world the way they're meant to.

It's fucking true!

Before I wrote that post, I just didn't think I was allowed to say — or even think — it yet.

I was unconsciously assuming I needed some elusive permission before I could stand in the truth of the unique and valuable approach I have to offer to an *industry,* not just a quiet little corner of the internet.

Oh. My. Fucking. God.

Here's the truth babe, no human authority is here to give anyone permission to be an industry leader or to tell anyone that their work is valuable.

You simply decide you have a contribution to make — and make it, whether the world puts you on a podium or not.

That's actually how one becomes an industry leader — they have something to share, and they back it. They see it and own it before anyone else does.

All a-fucking-long *you're the one* that's had the power to grant yourself permission to do the thing you want — to *be* the person you want to be.

The permission slip was in your motherfucking pocket the whole time.

You *are* the daddy.

Initiate This Code: Give Yourself the Slip

Babe, it's time to give yourself the slip for what's in your heart. Stop waiting for Prince Charming. He's not coming. It's time to place your own crown. It's time to make your soul calling your authority.

Step 1: See it
Put your current reality, doubts about your capabilities, and all sense of limitation aside for a moment — let yourself wander

into sweet imagination land where you can be, do, or have anything.

It's your turn to do the writing prompt. I've switched up "taking over" to "revolutionising" for the purposes of this exercise, but you can do either. Start off writing:

How I'm revolutionising the X industry in [year]...

Write for five minutes.
Free flow, from the heart, make it up.

Step 2: Be her now
What if you gave yourself permission to be that person *now*? What if you assumed that's actually your divinely ordered role in life — you're just still in the early stages of it?

How would you act?
How would you hold yourself?
What would you do?

Step 3: Act like it
There's a permission slip in your pocket.
Give it to yourself.

❖ Dive Deeper on the Podcast

If you want to unpack where you're waiting for permission to be/ do/ have in your life, and exactly what it means to give that permission to yourself... then join me in the podcast episode below.

> *Episode 153: Stop waiting for permission & how to give it to yourself* — from the ***Money, Sex, Business & Awakening Podcast***.
>
> **Listen here:** *beunacceptablebook.com/podcast-153*

It's you — it was always you.

You are the one.

Permission? *You never needed it.*

Or rather — you already had it. It's time to wake up to that truth and take your throne.

Next up on the chopping block of truth?

I'm going to show you how to turn your fears into gateways — ones that lead you straight back to your heart, your vision, and the fire to move.

CODE FIVE
Eat Your Fucking Fear for Breakfast

Break open to bliss.

ONE OF MY EARLIEST MENTORS said something that stuck with me — *I will eat this shame for breakfast.*

She was sharing that no matter how much healing you do, you'll never be fully *healed*. The same feelings of pain or disconnection will rise again — and when they do? Your only job is to feel them.

On the day she was sharing this, she was telling us that in her practice that morning, she'd found a whole ocean of shame inside herself.

She thought, *Fuck, how, after all these years, do I still have all this shame inside me?*

It never fully goes away, and it's not meant to. She said, after that initial thought, she just opened herself to meeting it *all*.

"Give it to me", she said. *"I'll be with anything. I can feel it all. I will eat this shame for breakfast."*

She went on to say that your ultimate power in life comes from your ability to be with anything — any thoughts, any feelings, any pain — and not need it to go away.

Over the years, I've found nothing to be truer.

That is what real mastery looks like.

Come at me, yo, I will fucking eat it all up. I can be with anything.

And that's what I want to offer you when it comes to fear.

Nothing sends the life you're meant to live to that damn graveyard faster than resisting the potential outcomes you fear.

And here's why:

When your brain perceives that going for what you want puts you at risk of something you've decided absolutely cannot happen, you won't be able to take action — not powerful, direct action anyway. Maybe some inessential, fluff-around action.

You can't actually reach your end result, because you're not open to the threats your ego perceives might appear along the way — or at the destination.

Your ego is always asking, *"What might happen if we do this? Will we survive? Or will we be hurt, rejected, or even outcast?"*

It's not basing that question on your true power, the opportunity in front of you, or the infinite wisdom of your higher self — it's projecting from the you that once felt powerless in a big, unpredictable world.

Not very helpful.

At the end of 2021, I decided to shift my 1:1 coaching model from a month-to-month setup to a twelve-month container *and* raise my rate at the same time.

At that point, I had four private clients on this month-to-month subscription model, three of whom had already been with me for over a year.

But I was so afraid to make the switch and really wanting to chicken out on implementing it with current clients.

I knew in my heart this new offer would better serve them — as well as my business (that paradox again) — but I had an overwhelming fear they'd think I was doing something bad.

My fear was that they'd stop liking me, stop working with me, and I'd lose the income I relied on.

In other words, I was afraid of what I might lose — approval and security.

If I remained unwilling to lose what I had, I wouldn't have been able to take action on this desire.

So I got vulnerable.

I made peace with my most feared outcome: *they all hate me, end coaching with me, and I lose one of my main sources of steady income.*

It was uncomfortable.

So here's what I did. I imagined that exact scenario playing out *and* imagined completely allowing it. I stopped resisting it as a possibility and instead, embraced it wholeheartedly as a possibility.

Not what I wanted, not what I was going for — but a possibility in among the infinite number of possibilities.

As soon as I let go and opened to it, my body softened, *and I felt my heart open.*

That outcome wasn't what I wanted, but if it happens — okay, I'll deal with that.

This is already awesome, but if you want to *really* open your consciousness way up so that fear isn't curbing and toning down your behaviour anymore, there's one more step... one more level:

Imagining the worst-case scenario continuing to unfold, after this first one, *for the rest of your life.*

To do this, I imagined the first feared outcome again — losing all my clients, they all hate me, etc. — then I imagined the worst thing that could happen after that, and after that, and after that, and after that... You get the idea.

For me this continued something like this: no one new signing up to coach with me, my whole audience thinking I was a bad person, and my whole business and life crumbling to the point of me moving back to live with my parents and work on their farm *forever.*

It's extreme, I know. But going there is necessary to free yourself and your energy to act on your truth.

Once I allowed it all, I felt that incredible freedom open up. I could finally just do what I wanted. This is because somewhere in the back of my mind, I was no longer trying to protect myself against something my ego thought could happen if I took action on my truth and towards my dreams.

I think it's important that I point out — sometimes this second level is very intense for your ego to face, and just like in *Celebrating How Gloriously Wrong You Are*, it can take some work to die to this thing, even though it's all just happening in your imagination.

I've had clients that go back into resistance to the first fear because their ego freaks out about this *even worse* thing to happen.

But I'm telling you, freedom is on the other side if you stay with it, breathe through it, and keep letting it be a possibility.

Remember, this is all just in your imagination. It's all about freeing up the energy in your consciousness. And the irony is, when you allow what you fear, it becomes much less likely to happen — but that's for another book.

Once I made peace with everything possibly going to shit, I acted on this change to my coaching model — *terrified*.

I had growing sweat patches as I told each client about the change and asked if they wanted to continue in a twelve-month container with me, *at a higher rate.*

One by one, I got, "*Yes, absolutely — that's so exciting, and even better! Sign me up.*"

My jaw dropped.

Yes? You're excited? You see it'll be better for you too — and I'm not just a bad person?

Three out of four signed on for the twelve-months.

And then get this...

... I opened the offer publicly — and within a couple of weeks, three more people I hadn't coached before signed up.

What. The. Actual. Fuck.

More people actually started coaching with me once I uplevelled my coaching model!

This shows you that the voice of fear is never telling the truth of a) the potential or b) what's best.

Making this change in my business changed everything. I could finally focus on serving, not surviving month to month. My work went deeper because my clients were committed for the long term. The results got bigger. And I was able to create more entry level programs for people in my audience.

All because I got *vulnerable* to the possibility that my deepest fear might actually happen... and acted in openness to that possibility.

This is how you *eat your fear for breakfast*.

Not by pretending it's not there.
Not by shoving it under the carpet.
Not by gaslighting yourself with positive thinking.
Not by trying to convince yourself it won't happen.

But by fully and completely opening yourself to it.

By dying to it.

By letting it be a risk you're willing to take, because your heart matters more than the illusion of safety.

You've changed masters, remember?

You're no longer devoted to survival — you're devoted to the Holy, Hot Service of Worshipping Your Heart. Your true authority. Your new altar.

Because the real daily nourishment isn't kale or cacao — it's the fear you're willing to digest.

Most people will never go there.

But the woman with self-mastery kneeling at the altar of her soul's path?

She goes there.
She allows it all.
She feels it all.

And she *Eats Her Fucking Fear for Breakfast.*

Initiate This Code: Feast on Your Fear

And now it's time for you to go there. You're ready. It's time to pull out that thorn and transmute your unconscious terror of attack, failure, or demise into an open heart that welcomes all — walks through the fire — and says, *"Is that all you've got?"* Quiver.

Step 1: The thing
What's something you want to do that you're not doing? Maybe it's something that's been sitting on your to-do list for six months... and it's still there.

Write it down.

Step 2: The fear
What are you afraid might happen if you do it? *The worst case scenario.*

Write it down.

Step 3: Eat it
Take a moment with your eyes closed and imagine that worst case scenario happening.

What do you see happening?
How do you feel?
What do you lose because of it?

In your imagination, allow that scenario to unfold, letting go of trying to stop it or control it. Full surrender. Just be with it.

What do you notice?

> ❖ **Dive Deeper on the Podcast**
>
> If you want to explore this process more deeply, you're in luck! Because I have a podcast episode I'm *always* sending people to that takes you through doing this process in more depth. It's honestly one of the most useful and go-back-to episodes on my podcast — I highly recommend listening and saving it!
>
> *Episode 22: The power of vulnerability in getting unstuck & creating what you love — from the* **Money, Sex, Business & Awakening Podcast**.
>
> **Listen here:** *beunacceptablebook.com/podcast-22*

I am so damn proud of you.

That right there — that's what it means to walk *The Divinely Wild Path of Being Unacceptable.*

Remember, the feared outcome you're opening yourself up to isn't what you want, it's not what you're going for — but when you allow the possibility of it, you free yourself from it.

Forget green juice and affirmations — have you eaten your fear today?

This is what it means to choose devotion over fear.

This is what it *really* means to choose love.

What's left once you've faced your fear and chosen your heart?

Turning up the volume on who you really are — which is exactly what our final Code is here to help you do. I think you're going to love it.

CODE SIX
Tone It Up

Be the fucking weirdo you are.

I was originally going to complete this book after the five Codes we've already covered, but as I was writing the last one, it became obvious — *there's one more step.*

We can thank my client Simone for this one.

The phrase came through in one of our sessions when I was tuning in to her next step towards one of her visions.

"Tone it up, Simone."

And it stuck.

Simone is an iconic, extra, opulent, stylish artist — but she'd been half-hiding that brilliance.

At Burning Man? It's all good.

Among family and friends? The voice creeps in — *Tone it down, Simone. Don't be too much. They'll think you're weird.*

She *is* weird — wonderfully over the top and visually decadent kinda weird. It's what makes her iconic. To cut that off is to water down the very essence that makes Simone, Simone and her art, art.

Our ego thinks that to be accepted, we have to fit in and be like everyone else.

Through our sweet innocent childhoods, we're wounded against what makes us different, but the truth is, it's what makes us different that makes us attractive — to the people we have true resonance with anyway, which is who you're here to be with in life and serve.

You think your difference makes you a freak, but it's your difference that *makes you special*. It makes you HOT. It makes you magnetic.

We want to hide parts of ourselves in order to be accepted by the world, but the very things we're here to be recognised for are the very things we hide.

For years, I tried to play the game of *acceptability*, from toning myself down to hiding entire parts of myself. Every time I did, things got harder. I had to push harder and force more just to fit in enough to get by.

But when I stopped trying to be anything other than exactly who I am and exactly where I am in life — raw, unfiltered, whole, and complete *now* — everything opened up.

Clients flowed in. Money flowed in. Support in every way I needed flowed in — sometimes in the most miraculous and unpredictable ways.

Life met me where I was — not where I was pretending to be.

Turns out, the real me is a damn magnet.

And the real *you* is a damn magnet, too.

The more you die to who you *think* you need to be to succeed in the world, the more life rushes in to support you.

The more you let-the-fuck-go of trying to be anything other than exactly who you are *right now* — all your weirdness and fucked-up-ness included — the more you receive.

It's another paradox.

That's what it means to *Tone It Up*.

It's being the real you, fully and unapologetically.

It's standing naked in the truth that you don't need to bend, morph, or shrink for anyone to be not only *valid*, but to *thrive* in life.

In fact, THAT is your gateway TO thriving.

Yes, you might be rejected. You might lose approval from sources you're used to getting it from. You might lose many things.

But you'll gain everything *you're meant for*.

You'll gain freedom, aliveness, vitality, magic, and authentic connection with the people you're inherently connected to — your true friends, chosen family and the soul community you're here to serve.

You'll gain true love in life.

Is that something you're willing to lose everything you have for?

To reach your death bed lit-up with the joy, satisfaction, and infinite gratitude of knowing you left no stone unturned, no part of yourself unexpressed, no song unsung, and no part of life unexplored?

You stopped being a beige carbon copy, and you chose to shine in all your glory.

You stopped being *acceptable*, and you lived the *Wildly Divine* and *Divinely Wild Path of Being Unacceptable:*

The place where soul dreams actualise, fortunes are found, and the gold in your heart is revealed to the world... as well as to yourself.

Is that worth risking daddy's approval for?
Is that worth risking people on the internet thinking you're an idiot?
Is that worth risking your high school friends thinking you've lost the plot?
Is that worth risking your relationship? The safe life you've built? The circles you want to belong in? The sense of security and control in your life?

Only you can decide what you make your life about.

If you dare to live the life you're meant for, it's time to *Tone It Up*.

Initiate This Code: Too Much and Here for It

Your final reclamation for this book? Fuck toning yourself down — let's tone it up, baby. Say good-the-fuck-bye to dimming your energy, making yourself more palatable for the world, and curbing your wild essence because you're afraid of being too much. That behaviour ends today.

Step 1: Find it
Get out your journal and pen. I want you journal for three minutes on the following prompt:

Where in your life are you toning yourself down, playing safe, or self-editing to make yourself more acceptable, normal, uncontroversial, and approved of in all your social environments?

Step 2: What are you suppressing?
Next, journal for three minutes on the following prompt:

Imagine it was not only wildly safe to be all of you — wild, raw, passionate, messy, and completely uninhibited — but also actually really attractive and exactly what made you really "fit in" where you're supposed to in the world.

What would you do differently?
What would you "let out"?

Where would you "let go"?
What would you "let yourself do"?
What intensity, craziness, or freakishness would you "let yourself be"?

Step 3: Free yourself
Based on what you've revealed from Step 1 and Step 2 — what's your obvious next step to *Tone It Up* in your life?

Write it down.
Do you dare do it?

> ❖ **Dive Deeper on the Podcast**
>
> If you need some more convincing that the way to serve your ultimate impact in the world *is* to embrace all of what makes you different, quirky, and weird, join me on the podcast for the episode below.
>
> *Episode 101: Why you *must* be your quirky-ass, weird self for your business to grow — from the* **Money, Sex, Business & Awakening Podcast**.
>
> **Listen here:** *beunacceptablebook.com/podcast-101*

And that's our six Codes, babe.

Now's the time to *live* them.

Let's recap, and then — if you dare — join me for a 30-day experience to embody everything you've just awakened and more.

The Be Unacceptable Codes

IT'S TIME TO WALK THE Divinely Wild Path of Being Unacceptable — *and dare to live the life you're meant for.* May these Codes support you in that pursuit.

1. *The Holy Hot Service of Self-Worship*

2. *Feel Unworthy and Do It Anyway*

3. *Celebrate How Gloriously Wrong You Are*

4. *You Are the Permission You've Been Waiting For*

5. *Eat Your Fucking Fear for Breakfast*

6. *Tone It Up*

Write them down.
Put them on the fridge.
Commit them to memory and repeat them to yourself in the moments you need their medicine.

They are medicine. I've specifically designed each Code to be something memorable that you can say to yourself all throughout the day.

I want you to take a moment to seriously imagine something: If you were to take on and apply these Codes wholeheartedly from today, every day, *what do you imagine would be different in your life after six months? A year? Five years?*

Don't let this be just an inspiring book you read once.

Let it be the book that changed the direction of your life and the level you're letting yourself play at — let it be a book that helped you take the reins and shine in the way you were always meant to.

The *genius idea graveyard* is calling — it has things that belong to you, and it says you're ready to take them back.

Go out there and *Be Unacceptable*.

Your Next Dare

The Be Unacceptable 30-Day Challenge

WHILE I WAS WRITING THIS book, I had a download — *what if I had a way to help you to live these Codes, not just read them?*

We all know it's one thing to read a great book that makes you laugh, cry, and feel disarmingly seen — but it's another to make what you've learned stick for more than a week once the inspiration wears off, and even be remembered for more than a few months.

I want to see you WIN. I want to see you on my newsfeed sharing how you unlocked the success you always saw for yourself. So, how can I help this stick and make that day inevitable?

The Be Unacceptable 30-Day Challenge.

This is the next step after reading this book — 30 days of daily prompts, reflections, and actions to help you wake up from your spells, apply the Code, and live boldly, bravely, and unapologetically as the woman you came here to be.

It takes the Codes you've learned out of theory and shows you exactly how to *live* them.

Normally **$111**, but as a book reader, you have a special code to join for only **$22.**

Babe, it's basically free, if you've resonated with what I've shared, do not NOT take this step.

The time is now, you'll never feel ready, changing your life comes down to choosing something different *today*.

Use code **BOOK22** at checkout to claim your special price.

This is the ultimate way to put everything we've covered into practice —

simple, potent, step-by-step prompts to ignite your *Unacceptable Path*.

Do you dare take the next step?

If you do this for 30 days, you won't just understand the Codes — they'll land, stick, and become your new way of life.

Join here:
beunacceptablebook.com/challenge

Or scan the QR code below.

Scan me

Book Closing

YOU WERE BORN FOR GREATNESS — your *unique* Greatness, not what the world labels respectable or worthy.

You've felt the calling of your heart. You know there's more to life than you're living right now, there's more for *you*, even if where you are right now is already something you once only dreamed of.

There's another exponentially greater level of what you're capable of and what you're here to experience — your soul service, creativity, abundance, and magic.

Not because you're not enough yet and not because your life isn't already an amazing blessing — but because your heart has more to give and you want to reach your deathbed knowing that you went all out and wholeheartedly *gave it*.

And, you have an illusion. You have an ego that casts spells on your mind. It whispers limits, replays old meanings, and projects the same fear onto whatever matters most right now.

It's not a flaw of your being — it's a feature. A safety mechanism running on old information. You just need to understand the truth of this and how to take the wheel again.

The *Codes* are your new set of tools to do that — they're keys to wake you up from the illusions your ego lulls you into and the sweet terrors of your wrongness it whispers in your ear. Use them. Live them. Breathe them.

Be relentless in applying them. Everytime you're triggered. Everytime your brain wants to spiral. Everytime you feel super fucked-up... *What do the Codes say? Which one do you need to apply?*

You *are* meant for more. And you won't find it playing *acceptable*.

You'll find it walking the *Divinely Wild Path of Being Unacceptable* — devoted, alive, un-fuck-with-able and free.

This book is my offering to you, and to the feminine. *May we rise.*

Now go — Be Unacceptable.

Dare to live the life you're meant for.

Epilogue
The Unacceptable Path

(Written 1 September 2018)

WHILE I WAS WRITING CODE Four — *You Are the Permission You've Been Waiting For* chapter — I found this piece I'd written offhand in my notes app, dated September 1st, 2018. I had completely forgotten writing it and never published it. Yet when I read it, I saw that I was always meant to write this book.

The Unacceptable Path

You're not here for ordinary,
you're here for extraordinary.

You didn't come into this world to follow the rules,
you came to carve your own path.

You didn't come to fall in line,
you came to lead a movement.

And now is the time.

They told you, you couldn't do it,
they told you to sign on the dotted line.
They told you to take a job. To play it safe.

But now is a time of awakening,
of remembering,
your true power,
and your true nature.

Awaken and remember,
you are a creator.

Every structure, every system,
every way that our culture does things,
was decided by someone no greater than you.

You get to decide what you want,
the time is now,
it's up to you.

Everything starts with a decision.
and the courage to follow through.

You must commit,
every day,
every time you fall off the bandwagon,
to get back on,
in pursuit of your vision.

This journey,
is not an overnight manifestation.

*It is a lifelong unfolding of self-discovery and self-realisation,
and you need to choose all of it.*

*Embark on this journey,
write the next chapter in your story,
don't let someone else write it for you,
don't let your fears write it for you.*

*Listen for the clues,
feel for the nudges,
and stay steady to your path.*

*There will be times when you feel like nothing is going right,
that this is all a joke,
that none of it's true,
that you're not a creator.*

*There will be times,
you question if you were tricked,
into believing,
that the world could be yours.*

*This is where your work begins, my friend.
This is where you remember.*

*Again and again,
you remember,
you were never ordinary,
and you always were,
the creator.*

About the Author

ALEX HARVEY IS AN AUTHOR, coach, entrepreneur, and creator devoted to waking women up to who the fuck they are, and reclaim the power of their once-suppressed feminine nature.

Known for her bold, sassy, raw, and deeply embodied approach, Alex guides women beyond the surface-level fluff of personal development to uncover their true spiritual gifts and live the life they're meant for. Her work fuses the principles of alchemy, mind science, and sacred sexuality to empower women to become the unapologetic industry-shaping leaders they were born to be.

She's the founder of **The Modern Woman Academy**, creator of **The Feminine Alchemy Method**, and founder of the fashion and pleasure brand **Dare The Label** — all extensions of her core mission: to help women unlock their wild, unfiltered expression in the world.

Based in Bali, when she's not creating, coaching, or writing, Alex can be found lifting heavy things, being lifted into the air by other humans, dancing, lost in sensual rapture, or exploring this beautiful world.

Be Unacceptable is the first book in her body of teachings — a manifesto for women ready to break free of the shackles their bound by in their own mind and dare to live the life they're meant for.

Where you can find Alex

- **On Her Podcast:** Money Sex Business & Awakening

- **On Instagram:** @alexh.co

- **Email:** hello@themodernwoman.academy

- **Coaching Academy Website:** themodernwoman.academy

- **Dare The Label Website:** darethelabel.co

- **Dare The Label Instagram:** @darethelabel.co

Also by Alex Harvey

Make Money Want You
A short and powerful eBook sharing the 5 wealth principles no one ever taught you that will enable you to grow your income and wealth, doing the work you love.

Available at **makemoneywantyou.com**

Curated Companion

Podcast Episodes to Compliment This Book

ALL EPISODES CAN BE FOUND on the **Money Sex Business & Awakening** podcast.

Available on Spotify, Apple Podcast, iHeartRadio, and anywhere you listen to podcasts.

- Episode 150: Why I've been avoiding writing my book for two years

- Episode 140: What you think is happening - isn't happening

- Episode 135: Ok, you're taking action but are you turned on?

- Episode 130: How to find your purpose (the truth no one talks about)

- Episode 129: How to live your you *highest vibration*

- Episode 128: Break free from *Good Girl Conditioning*: The 10x programs that keep you small

- Episode 125: The Masculine & Feminine of Manifesting - are you missing one?

- Episode 101: Why you *must* be your quirky-ass, weird self for your business to grow

- Episode 99: "No one wants my offers" - the significance wound

- Episode 89: Eating shame for breakfast (in your biz)

Go to this URL for instant access to this curated list: **beunacceptablebook.com/podcast**

Thank You

To my Mum for being a rock in my life and for your unconditional love. Knowing I always have a home to come back to if I really do fuck everything up has given me so much strength through my fear. But most of all, feeling seen by you in my Greatness in these last years is one of the biggest gifts I've been given.

To my Dad who has taught me so much in life, including that it's okay to take a path no one else sees or believes in, it's okay to do things differently from everyone else, it's okay to be a loner for both of those thing, it's okay to go through periods of "failure" it's part of taking risks in life, and that no matter what, you can always find solutions.

To my 1:1 and mastermind clients who enthusiastically receive my wisdom and apply my methods and theories as they land. The fact that you all deeply feel the resonance with what comes through me and embrace it wholeheartedly has truly allowed this body of work to come together. This book absolutely would not exist without you. In particular to Alyce, Amber, Ambre, Jolien, and Simone who were there, in orgasmic "yes" as I finally let it all out.

To all my clients who've allowed me to use stories or your exact words to help bring to life the concepts I've shared in this book. Thank you for your generosity and service to this book.

To my coach and mentor William Whitecloud, I will — like you once said — kiss your feet when I see you next. The wisdom you've passed on to me is so profound and I wouldn't be the woman I am today without your guidance. Your generosity of heart and spirit has given me an example of service like I had never known. I am eternally grateful for everything you've taught me — it's the real deal.

To Madeline Kossin for your sales challenge that gave me a slap and woke me up to where I was still suppressing my power and authority.

To my friend Miranda, who agreed to have the book launch for this book at your house, just thank you. Thank you for the past four years of voice notes, support, shared contemplation of Alchemy and of feminine nature. Your support over these years has been everything.

To anyone who's ever taken any of my programs over the years — it's been an absolute honour to serve you. You've been part of this book coming to life too. Thank you for trusting my guidance.

To everyone who reads my content on social media — thank you, I love you, you're part of this too.

And to you, reading this book — I hope it's given you something you'll take with you for the rest of your life. Thank you for receiving my soul's expression, my art.

If You Loved This Book...

IF THIS BOOK MOVED YOU, touched your heart, opened something inside you, or just made you laugh and feel deeply seen, I'd *love* to hear from you. And if it awakened you in some way, please pass the flame. The world needs more women remembering who the fuck they are and the power that they have to create their dreams.

Here are four simple ways you can do that — and truly, from the bottom of my heart, thank you if you choose to do any of them:

1. Leave a review on Amazon

One of the most powerful ways to both share your reflections and help spread this work is by leaving a review on Amazon. It means so much and is an incredible act of support.

Here's how:
Head over to **Amazon.com**, search *Be Unacceptable*, open the listing, scroll to the bottom, and click **"Write a customer review."** If you've purchased anything from Amazon in the last

12-months, you'll be eligible to leave one (if not, you might need to make a small purchase first).

2. Give a copy to a friend

If you've finished your copy, pass it on to someone who needs it. Or — if you don't want to part with your copy (I get it!) — grab a few extras to gift.

You can order additional copies anytime at **beunacceptablebook.com.**

Gifting this book is one of the most beautiful ways to help me get this message into the hearts and hands of more women who need it.

3. Send me a message on Instagram (or an email)

I would *adore* hearing from you personally — and I'll probably cry. Send me a message on Instagram and tell me what you loved, what touched your heart, or how this book has impacted you — it'll honestly make my day.

Find the book Instagram **@beunacceptable** and me, Alex, at **@alexh.co** . Or, if you're not on Instagram, you can always reach me via email with this address: **hello@themodernwoman.academy.**

4. Share a photo

Snap a photo of you with the book, or your favourite quote, share it on your social media and tag me (IG handles are **@beunacceptable** and **@alexh.co**) + use the hashtag #beunacceptable. Or alternatively, send me the photo directly in the DM's.

Seeing you reading, laughing, crying, or underlining your favourite parts fills my heart to bursting — and every share helps this movement grow.

Thank you for being here, for reading, for daring, for remembering.

Order Copies of This Book

To order copies of this book, go to **beunacceptablebook.com**

or scan the QR code below.

Scan me

www.ingramcontent.com/pod-product-compliance
Lightning Source LLC
Chambersburg PA
CBHW020528080526
44583CB00013B/777